STICKS & STONES &
ONCE BROKEN BONES

MOLD YOUR **PERCEPTION**
TRANSFORM YOUR **MINDSET**
AND DISCOVER **HOPE** THROUGH
THE POWER OF **PERSEVERANCE**

Alejandro,
    Thank you for allowing me to share a piece of me with you. May God continue to bless you as you persevere with hope!

AMBER NOELLE

Amber Noelle

AUTHOR ACADEMY elite

Copyright © 2016 Amber Noelle

All rights reserved.

Published by Author Academy Elite
P.O. Box 43, Powell, OH 43035

www.AuthorAcademyElite.com

All rights reserved. No part of this publication may be reproduced, stored in a retrieval system, or transmitted in any form or by any means—for example, electronic, photocopy, recording—without the prior written permission of the publisher. The only exception is brief quotations in printed reviews.

Unless otherwise noted, Scripture quotations are from the Holy Bible, New International Version®. NIV®.

Photography by Danielle Reardon
Copy Editing/Proofreading by William K. Weber

For my children—Justin, John, and Julia.
You are my inspiration. I love you forever and always.

CONTENTS

Foreword by: Kary Oberbrunner vii

PART I   SETTING THE STAGE

Chapter 1:   What Breaks Your Heart? 3
Chapter 2:   Inspiration 9
Chapter 3:   The Cast 21

PART II   PERCEPTION

Chapter 4:   WARNING: This is Going to Hurt 33
Prepare For a Beat-Down

Chapter 5:   A Trip Down Memory Lane 43
Let's Camp Out in the Past

Chapter 6:   A Little Further Now 53
Go Within—or Go Without

Chapter 7:   Valid 73
You and Your 'Feelings'

PART III   MINDSET

Chapter 8:   One Common Denominator 85
Owning Your Piece of the Pain

Chapter 9: In This Corner 97
    Guilt vs. Guilty

Chapter 10: False 'Facts' 117
    Can You Handle the Truth?

PART IV HOPE AND PERSEVERANCE

Chapter 11: Accept This Cancer 127
    The Promise of Blessing

Chapter 12: The Secret Passageway into Hope 143
    Surrender and Forgiveness

Chapter 13: Race with Horses 163
    The Course of Persistence, The Prize of Endurance

Chapter 14: So You Wanna Be A Freak? 175
    Persevering Through the Uncertainty

PART V THE THREE CHILDREN—*MY THREE CHILDREN*

FOREWORD

Have you ever imagined if your life could be different?
Have you ever wished you could rewrite your story?

What if you could?
You have a choice; you always have a choice.

With infectious vulnerability, Amber Noelle invites you into a story of her own brokenness. Throughout these pages you'll see yourself in a new way. Whether it's the allegory of the Toy Maker in chapter two or the scenes of promise found further in the story, you'll be pulled into a new way of believing what's possible.

As her story unfolds, you'll feel the hope that resides within her—hope for something more.

This more is what propels her to persevere through even the roughest of storms.

Amber challenges you along the way to join her on this journey of self-discovery and transformation. While she promises authenticity, she also assures you the path won't be easy. It may be downright painful. But it will be worth it, since every choice, every step, brings you closer to discovering more in your own story.

Author and life coach, Amber takes you on this journey of self-discovery, helping you to:

- address your brokenness while taking a trip down memory lane
- own your piece of the pain through identifying the one common denominator in your struggle
- overcome guilt and shame, putting them behind you once and for all
- find hope and develop the ability to persevere despite the sticks and stones that have seemingly broken you
- discover the more that's just on the other side of the finish line

Prepare to be challenged.
Prepare to be inspired.

But most of all, prepare to discover the more that you've been searching for your whole life. Join Amber on this journey, and begin to rewrite your story today.

Unleash your PERSEVERING spirit and embrace the MORE that awaits you.

—Kary Oberbrunner

- CEO of Redeem the Day and Igniting Souls; Co-founder of Author Academy Elite
- Author of Day Job to Dream Job, The Deeper Path, and Your Secret Name

Part I

SETTING THE STAGE

1

WHAT BREAKS YOUR HEART

What breaks your heart?

I was first asked this question, not personally, but while sitting in an auditorium full of people. The speaker was challenging the audience to really dig deep and discover their purpose. I thought about this question as I sat there that day, several years ago. And even now, as I sit in my comfy chair writing these words, I think of it again.

More recently, again, I heard a question asked. "Many years from now, what do you want people to line up and thank you for?" In other words, what do you want to be remembered by? In what way do you want your life to impact other people?

Each of these questions and many more like them center around discovering what you were created to do, who you were created to be, how your unique qualities and characteristics and talents and gifts can be fine-tuned to reveal a greater purpose for your life.

Through the last several years of my life, I have experienced moments—some little, almost forgettable moments; some big, unforgettable, mind-blowing moments. All of which have to do with these questions burning deep in my soul, desperately needing to be answered: *What is my purpose? What am I here for, created to be, meant to do?*

I sat in Panera Bread sipping on coffee and reading over my notes, my outline sketched out on paper, a business plan of sorts. I was waiting to meet with a man I had met years ago, a man who had grown to be a bit of a father figure to me, a mentor. He was a very attentive, very skilled listener. I had been looking forward to this day with great anticipation. I had another big idea and could not wait to share it with him.

What I had sketched out on paper was a plan to open up a coffee shop. But this was to be no ordinary coffee shop. I would call it the 'Creative Kafe.' Oh the ideas I had! Such a burning passion to serve others, to reach their hurting hearts. My plans for the Creative Kafe ranged from fundraising for underprivileged kids in the local community to hosting workshops for business leaders to incorporating a fitness studio. And I had every last detail of the interior sketched out in my head. I even had a logo designed. I was practically bursting at the seams with anticipation. I couldn't wait to set this plan into action, to start taking the steps to open up my Creative Kafe!

I had gotten there about an hour early. As I sat and went over all the details, I could hardly contain my excitement. I was so eager to share my plan with him, sure to see a big proud smile on his face, hear him give me his approval. I even imagined he would be so excited he'd want to be involved in the building of this great plan.

Finally, he walked through the door, right on time. Gave me a hug and sat down, ready to listen.

As I started talking, I immediately felt a sense of anxiety rush over me. I figured it was just the four cups of coffee I drank while waiting for his arrival. But as I began to reveal my great big idea, as I began sharing all the small details, I suddenly stopped. I said to him, "Ya know, I just don't feel like I can share any more of this with you. It feels wrong all of a sudden." After spending months thinking of this cafe—waking up in the middle of the night with another detail to jot down in my notebook; daydreaming of how it would look; picturing myself running this coffee shop that was to be far more than the usual simple, quiet coffee shop you see around street corners—I suddenly felt my heart sink. So after spending roughly half an hour talking and sharing, I just ... stopped.

My friend Gary reached across the table. He grabbed my hand. By now I was crying, feeling so overwhelmed with disappointment. He said to me, "Kiddo, this is not your purpose. You are searching in all the wrong places." He paused. Then he looked me dead in my eyes, now full of tears, and said, "You are to share your story. Write it down in your notebook: Mark my words—this is your calling, your purpose."

Man, oh man. My heart instantly sank. I had spent months pouring my heart and emotions into this Creative Kafe and dreaming of how I could serve and reach people. My world just blew up at that very moment. My *story*? Who in the world would want to hear my story? I had often described my life as a bunch of really crappy Lifetime movies balled up into one pathetic girl's life. Who would want to hear such a depressing story?

He went on to explain how he believed I was to deliver hope. He believed I had been given—or more accurately, more than given but blessed—with the obstacles I had overcome for a purpose much greater than a silly little cafe.

Gary was never one to sugarcoat anything, which was quite possibly why I gravitated toward him, why I respected his insight so much. He'd say it like it was, whether it left behind hurt feelings or a bruised ego. So while he burst my bubble that day at Panera Bread, he gave me something to think about that ultimately opened a door into discovering my purpose.

Before you turn the page to the next chapter of this book, I want to give you 'my word,' a promise from me to you. But before I do, let me be clear on a few things. I hold no doctorate degree. I have acquired nothing more than a simple associates degree in visual communications from a technical school that doesn't even exist anymore. Quite frankly, I'd consider myself to be an expert on not much of anything. That being said, I want to promise you that I will not pretend to be something I am not. I will not write or speak on anything as if I am an expert in areas I know very little about.

But what I will promise you is this: I will be authentic. I will be honest. I will be open and vulnerable with you. I will be nothing less than 'real.' I acknowledge that I am no greater than you. And … I will share my story with you, as my dear friend and mentor suggested. I will share with you what breaks my heart. And my purpose in doing so is to touch hurting souls, even if it's just one—maybe yours.

In addition to my promise of authenticity, I will promise you one more thing: I will not waste your valuable time. I respectfully request that if after reading the next chapter your heart doesn't break in some way, then you don't have to continue reading. Return the book to the store where you bought it and get your money back, or put it on your bookshelf for another day, or give it to someone else. If this next chapter doesn't resonate with you on some level, I don't want your valuable time to be wasted. Pick up another book and keep searching until a spark ignites you and you begin to tap into what breaks your heart.

2

INSPIRATION

During my season of self-discovery, I would often awaken at night with an intense urge to get out of bed, slip on my glasses, and start writing. A thought or idea would wake me up, and I'd have to jot it down before drifting back to sleep.

But one early morning was different from the rest. I woke up with a distinct feeling that I wouldn't be drifting back to sleep anytime soon. What was typically a quick five minutes turned into a few hours of writing. The experience was different too, because what transpired resulted in a short story, rather than just a few scribbled notes in a notebook I kept on my bedside table.

Now let me tell you that I believe in what some might call 'divine inspiration.' Simply put, what I experienced that particular morning while writing was not of my own consciousness. So I feel it's only fair to give credit where credit is due. I was simply the hand writing the words on paper, nothing more. An instrument, so to speak.

Which is why I feel compelled to share this short story that came to me at 3:30 one fateful morning, and that I leave it just exactly as it was—untainted, honest, unedited, with grammatical errors and all. It is raw and as real as the stinky-breath, crusty-eyed, pajama-clad, messy-haired person who wrote it that day.

So without further ado, I give you … what breaks my heart …

the TOYMAKER

Once upon a time...

There was once an orphanage. In it were many children, some very young, some old. But this story is about three children, once young, now growing older. Being brought to this orphanage as only infants, these children were naturally happy in their environment. Their caretakers, the men and women who tended to them daily, were kind, warm, and loving.

Then one day, an unusual excitement filled the orphanage. The children scampered from room to room, breathless, excited. "The Toy Maker is coming today! The Toy Maker is coming!"

Just moments later came the long awaited chime of the doorbell, and the children rushed downstairs. The three children, a bit timid, hand in hand, cautiously peered through the crowd, keeping a safe distance. They watched in amazement as this large man with messy hair, overgrown beard, and the largest hands they had ever seen reached into a large box. One by one, he pulled out a handcrafted toy for each of the children.

The children had never seen such an assortment of toys before, and each seemed to be crafted specifically for the child receiving it. But these three children could see something very unique from their distant position. Where the other children's focus was on the box full of splendor, these three children, from afar, were drawn to this large man's face. Surrounded by unruly hair and an unshaven face were the kindest brown eyes they had ever seen.

As the man reached into the box and handed each child a toy, the children noticed how he looked at each and every one of them. The other children never took notice, their focus only on the toy. But these three children noticed, and once they caught a glimpse of it, they couldn't help but stare into those big brown eyes. They had for the first time seen something different. Different than the loving, kind eyes of their caretakers. Different than what they had seen in each other's eyes for all these years.

Month after month, the Toy Maker visited. Again, the excitement. Again, the squealing. And again, the three children scampered downstairs to take it all in from a safe distance, as always. Each time the large man came, and after each new child in the orphanage received their toy, he folded down the corners of his box without ever saying a word, and lifted up the box carefully as if there was still something inside.

Then his gaze would fix on the three children who were huddled in the corner, just watching. And each time, month after month, the Toy Maker would pause, his big brown eyes almost disappearing as he smiled at the three children. Then he would simply nod, as if to say, "See you next month." The man never spoke a word for as long as the children could remember him coming. Likely no one ever noticed, as the focus was always on the big box of toys. But the three children noticed. They seemed to see only the man, with his big brown eyes, unruly hair, and kind smile.

Then one morning, the children woke to the same monthly excitement. The same squealing, the same scampering down the stairs, little bodies almost falling over one another in their rush. But today was different. The three children had decided together that the next time they hear the long awaited chime of the doorbell, they were going to step just a little closer, out of the safety of their corner and see for themselves—and see from the other children's perspective—what was in that box.

They had been watching as month after month, the man packed up his box, with something clearly still inside it. Maybe it was curiosity. More likely, it was this growing sense of loneliness they had come to know. For months, even years now, they had watched as each new child to the orphanage received a toy. This toy was all their own. This toy was by their side at all times. Somehow that same peculiar look they had seen in the

Toy Maker's deep brown eyes, they could clearly see in the eyes of these children. It was impossible to explain, but it was some sort of mixture of pure happiness, contentment, and security. The three children couldn't clearly pinpoint what exactly it was. They only knew they surely didn't have it. It wasn't the toy they desired near as much as it was the look in the other children's eyes. They wanted that same look, the same look the other children neglected to see in the Toy Maker's eyes.

But today was going to be different than the rest of the other days as the three children, hand in hand, crept closer and closer until they too were pressed up against the others, on tip-toes, trying to peer into that great big box of splendor. Soon the children all scampered away, new toy in hand, and there stood these three children, now only an arm's length away from the man. Up close, the man was so much bigger.

They looked up as the man quietly came down to his knees. He reached out his hands as he sat on the floor, inviting the children to come closer. Their hearts beating wildly from the overwhelming rush of emotion, the three children stepped closer, and the man wrapped them in his arms. He was strong, his hands huge, and he smelled how they would imagine a woodshop might smell like. He didn't say a word, just held them tightly until their little beating hearts slowed down, beating in rhythm with his.

Then as he reached into his box, pulling out only one toy, he spoke. "This toy," he said, "is for the three of you to share. It is special. It is unique. I made it myself. No other child has this same toy. I've been keeping it here in my box, hoping you would come ask for it." And with those few words, the only words they had ever heard the man speak, he stood up, looked down at them with the same big brown eyes—almost disappearing as his smile stretched from ear to ear, and quietly nodded at the children.

As the three children grew, though they played with other children, though they loved their caretakers, there was nothing that brought them comfort quite like their very own unique, special toy. They hadn't seen the Toy Maker in years. Each month, he came as scheduled. Each month, the new arrivals to the orphanage ran downstairs to greet him. The three children knew he was there, but they no longer had a need for him. Still, they would sit quietly upstairs with their toy, and just listen. Listening as if they were trying to hear the smile on the man's face as he nodded and walked out the door.

As the years passed by, the children continued to grow. Just as they had always done together, even as very small children, they would observe. They observed the other children around them. They observed the caretakers. And they began to see something they had never seen before.

As young children, they saw nothing but kindness and love and happiness, having no understanding of the environment they were in. But now that they were older, they started to notice that the children they once played with were walking out the door of the orphanage, one by one, into the hands of strangers. They started to notice that the caretakers weren't always smiling, they weren't always kind, and sometimes, they would leave, never to be seen again without even a goodbye.

The children started to feel emotions they had never experienced before. They felt angry, they felt resentful. They were scared and disappointed. They felt unworthy. The toy that once brought security and joy and comfort, being their only source of consistency, now became their outlet for release. The children began punching the toy when they felt angry, or whenever another child or caretaker would walk out the door, never to be seen again.

The toy took quite a beating. But what the children had never realized about this gift from the Toy Maker was that he designed this toy especially for them. They had often wondered, through the years, why some of the other children's toys were different from theirs. It was now, for the first time, that they could see why. This toy had a special addition. It had a spring. And each time they punched the toy, it sprang back up, still with the same consistent smile on its face. The children would beat on it one minute, and then the next they would hug it dearly. It was stained with tears, it was battered on the outside, and though still smiling, it appeared to be broken and even worthless. But the children loved it dearly. And because of its special feature they had failed to recognize for all those years, they loved it even more because of its ability to spring back up time and time again. They discovered a new appreciation for their toy, an appreciation many of the other children never discovered in their own toys.

Through this painful few years of discovery, the three children had begun to see others in a different light. They themselves would kneel down, look into the eyes of the other, much younger children in the orphanage, and hold them tight. The caretakers began to see something special, something unique, something intriguing in these three, now young adults, as they stopped from time to time to kindly look deep into their eyes and simply nod, as if to say, "Thank you for taking care of me, for being kind, for helping me." These three young adults began to see a light where, for a period of time, they could only see darkness. They chose to see in others what they had discovered in their toy. They chose to see the good in them, their own special gifts and uniqueness, and they began to see the good where others only saw the broken.

As the time was soon approaching for these three grown children to leave the orphanage, never having been adopted, never having left the isolated walls of their 'home,' they looked down at their toy. It had seen better years. The paint was faded, the exterior left something to be desired. Yet, they couldn't help but feel attached to it. Though never recognizing its true value or unique ability as young children, they couldn't help but reflect on that period of their life, now seeming so long ago, where through their own struggles they began to see just how resilient their toy could be. They loved it dearly.

Then they heard it. They had not even noticed the doorbell for years now, but as they sat there, their toy in hand, they heard the rush of tiny feet scampering past them to go meet the Toy Maker. The three children hadn't seen him in a very long time, or even stopped to think of him. But they stood to their feet, and quietly, so to not disrupt the joyous scene, tip-toed down the stairs. With their eyes fixed on the Toy Maker, they aimed to quietly slip into that same back corner where they had sat years ago, observing.

But today was different. Yes, today was different indeed. Just as the three children had nestled into their safe little corner, the Toy Maker fixed his own eyes on the three children. He instructed the anxious children at his feet to sit quietly and wait. With arms open wide, he ran to the three young adults, no longer little children, and threw his arms around them and wept. As they all wept together, the Toy Maker waited for their beating hearts to slow down into rhythm with his. He then looked at them with those same deep brown eyes, still unruly hair, still overgrown beard, still same woodshop smell, and he told of how he'd missed seeing their faces, how he'd missed their inquisitive little feet scampering over to the corner to watch from their safe zone.

Then he said, "My children, where is your toy?"

Their faces, which were filled with excitement just moments ago, now dulled. Their heads dropped as they reached behind and held up the toy the Toy Maker had crafted so carefully and uniquely for them. They explained how they had cherished it, but they had been rough on it sometimes, and how though they loved it and they hated it at times. With shame in their eyes, they lifted it up and handed it over to the Toy Maker.

The Toy Maker then asked them, "But through the years, did you discover the unique feature I designed in this toy?"

"Oh yes, the spring!" they answered. "But how did you know? How did you know that we would hurt it, that we would mistreat it? How did you know?"

The Toy Maker, with tears in his eyes, said, "Oh my children, this isn't just any old toy. I knew exactly what this toy would have to endure. I knew exactly what this toy would need to withstand. And so I designed this toy just for YOU. It was designed with strength, with perseverance. I designed it to consistently perform as it should through any circumstances. But this toy, before you came to discover its special design, provided you with comfort, with companionship, with love and with hope. And through the years, it has never once failed to love you."

Then the Toy Maker took the precious toy in his hands, and said, "What I designed for you, what I gave to you, is irreplaceable. I GAVE YOU A MOTHER."

He paused for a moment and explained as the three children looked confused. "My children, though happy and content for many years of your young life, you grew to see your surroundings through the eyes of those here much longer than you. You saw your life as if you were living in an orphanage, abandoned, left alone to suffer. All the while surrounded by the voices, the faces of other children, of other adults. You knew I was here, I came regularly, consistently, hoping, waiting for you to come to me. And when you finally took that brave step toward me, my own heart wept with happiness, as I had been carrying around this gift for you for a very long time. I created her and designed her a long time ago—she herself having been refined to acquire her special spring, knowing there would one day be three children, suffering and lost, that would need the exact unique gifts I had created her with."

When the three children had realized the worth of this worn-out, used toy, their faces hung with shame. But the Toy Maker again embraced the three children, and said with a warm and proud, confident smile, "Oh, not to worry, children. I will take her back to my shop and I will fix her up, good as new. I have wonderful plans for her. Her purpose has only just begun."

That very day, the three children gathered their few belongings, feeling a little lost without their mother. But what the Toy Maker had given them years ago now resided in their hearts. They were ready to venture out into the world, once as a unit of three, now as individuals even more powerful than three, because they now had the light of their mother, of their Maker, and each other radiating out of them. They were the few out of their 'orphanage' who were blessed with eyes to see, with ears to hear, and with hearts to feel the magnitude of the greatness that now resided in them—gifted to them by The Toy Maker.

3

THE CAST

I assume it's safe to say that since you are still reading this, the previous chapter resonated with you on some level. I wrote that story almost one year ago. And I've shared it with just a small handful of people. But what amazes me to this day is that whether it was the first time I'd read it or the fiftieth, as I just did, I still cry. Sounds crazy, right? I'm the one who wrote it. I know how the story goes. I've read it over and over. And yet, it stirs emotion in me as if I'm reading it for the first time, as if someone else wrote it.

What does that tell me, you ask? It's simple. This is what breaks my heart. And as I have been reminded several times throughout the last several years—sometimes very bluntly, sometimes in a more subtle manner—my purpose revolves around sharing my story.

What's interesting is that while I was working on this book for months, after being stuck for weeks on the same chapter, I had one of those *aha* moments. I started writing this book with the focus on how I can reach everyone who picks it up, how I can relate to everyone's hurts, everyone's struggle, everyone's damaged past. But suddenly, something rather obvious occurred to me. And so I decided to scrap all the work I had done and start completely over.

While there are parts of my story that many others can relate to, no one else on this planet has had the very same exact story as mine. And might I say, no one else on this planet has had the same exact story as yours, either. So how could I possibly reach everyone? I cannot. But I believe in my heart that if you finished reading The Toy Maker and you felt something tug at your heart, there's a piece of me that can relate to you. So I'll share my story with you with the belief that God will stir something within you as He has in me.

> What makes your story unique? What makes the difference between two people who have experienced the same exact thing? Perception. That is what sets you apart from me, what sets me apart from you. Not the 'what' in the experience, but the 'how' in the experience. It's not, 'what has happened to me,' but 'how do I perceive what has happened to me.'

What makes the difference between two people who have experienced the same exact thing? **Perception.**

Now let me ask you this: What do you want your story to be?

If you could rewrite your past, if you could take away the pain you've experienced, if you could rewrite the disease, rewrite the lost job, rewrite the failed marriage, the wayward child, the accident, the abuse, the dad who walked out on you, the depression ... would you? Of course. You'd be crazy not to if given the chance to rewrite your story. You'd be crazy to leave it just as it is.

But what if I told you that you truly *can* rewrite your story? What if I told you that the secret to rewriting your story all lies in your *perception*? In other words, if you suddenly begin to see your situation as something entirely different from what it actually is.

I can quite vividly remember a 'not so pleasant discussion' I was having with someone a few years back. I remember him saying to me, matter-of-factly, "You're delusional." He had been trying to convince me of something, something he felt to be true of me. Yet, I saw it differently. Delusional? Maybe. I never claimed to be sane! And while there may have been pieces of his assessment to be true, the way I perceived it to be true was no less factual than his own perception. Same topic. Same discussion. Same experience. Different perception.

The three orphaned children spent their entire childhood perceiving they were lost and abandoned siblings confined to the walls of an orphanage. In fact, as we discover in the last part of their childhood, they were anything but alone. But what makes the difference between what was true reality and what was true to them? Perception.

Since you are still reading, I want to make one more promise to you. You already possess the wisdom, the ability, the strength to write the rest of your story any way you want. That's right, you do. And I want to provide some practical steps to help you tap into that strength and that wisdom to alter your perception.

To be clear, as I confessed earlier in the first chapter, I am no expert in much of anything. The only thing I can speak of with certainty, with clarity, and with confidence is my own story. Having reminded you of that, I would also like to make a deal with you.

I will be vulnerable. I will openly invite you into my story and introduce you to the cast of "The Toy Maker" as they relate to my own life, with the intent to instill in you a will to persevere and to shine even just a small ray of hope into your own life, your own story. What I ask of you in exchange is that you do the same. You need not share with any one person, but for me to be able to hold up my end of the deal, you will have to agree to become vulnerable as well. You must be honest with yourself, if with no one else. You will be required to dig deep to where the pain is almost unbearable. You will experience even more pain and discomfort throughout this process, but you will discover something absolutely invaluable—the courage and strength to change the course of your story.

THE CAST

The Three Children

Inquisitive little buggers, aren't they? Can't you just picture them anxiously waiting for the next visit from the Toy Maker? But not with the same purpose as the other children did. Rather, it would seem that curiosity was what drew these children to scamper downstairs, and then quickly retreat to their safe corner to watch. They took in every last detail—the sound of chatter coming from the impatient children as they crowded around the large box of toys; the unfamiliar smell of a workshop as it traveled across the room, which came from the large man's hands as he reached across the children and handed them their gifts one by one; the nervous excitement rushing through their little bodies as they fought back the urge to rush over and get a closer look. The safety of their corner, as if they had become invisible, allowing them to take it all in as if in slow motion.

But the one detail that, time after time, seemed to put these three inquisitive children in a trance was the deep brown eyes of this large, unkempt, peculiar man. The way he intently looked at each of the children, as if he was giving them something so much more than just a wooden toy. It was almost as if through his big brown eyes he was transferring something directly to the hearts of those other children, something they couldn't quite put their finger on.

But it's what brought them scampering back downstairs, back into their safe corner, every single time they heard the familiar chime of the doorbell.

You have to wonder, why did these three behave so differently from the rest of the children? What was it that made them so timid, why did they never seem to leave one another's side? Was it insecurity? Fear? Or perhaps just their cautious nature?

The Toy Maker

The Toy Maker. Where to start ... What stands out to you as most impressive about this man?

What stands out to me most, I'd have to admit, is the fact that every single time he returned to visit the children of the orphanage, he would bring with him a specially crafted toy, made with unique specifications. And at every visit, he would peer at the three children in the corner, smile and nod his head, and then lift the once-heavy box, now much lighter, holding only one lonely toy. He would turn his back to leave without saying a word, only to return again, carrying with him the same toy, patiently waiting for the three children's curiosity to triumph over their fear.

He never pressured the children. But he certainly tapped into their inquisitive characters. You'd think he could have washed up before he came to visit them, so that maybe his hands and clothing wouldn't smell of the workshop. Perhaps he could have combed his hair, or even shaved. But why did he remain so quiet? Why did he make a point to look right through the children as he handed them their toys? And why did he keep leaving with something clearly still rattling around in that big box? Didn't he speak? Why didn't he utter even a single word to any of the excited children falling over one another, crowding around at his feet?

Sly and clever man, that Toy Maker. I have to believe he knew exactly what he was doing.

The Toy

You know the Toy probably better than anyone. You're familiar with the heartwarming feeling of being needed, of being wanted, of being loved. You may have experienced these indescribably incredible feelings to a great degree, from a great many people throughout your story. You may have only experienced it once or twice, quite possibly for just a fleeting moment. But what a grand feeling it is to know you're providing someone with comfort, with joy, with companionship, with love, with acceptance.

Then the storm hits. It rages on without any signs of relief. The same source that so willingly accepted your love and your comfort now becomes a source of resentment, of contempt, of anger, or ridicule. Your entire world, your entire purpose, has revolved around providing, around giving, around fulfillment. And now, you find yourself being pelted with hail, the deafening thunder shaking you to your very core, and all the while you still manage to spring back up to give again, to provide again, to fulfill again. Only to endure storm after storm.

You take a beating. You don't look so hot on the outside anymore, and you feel even worse on the inside. Yet your face suggests a smile. Yet you spring back up time after time. Why? Because you were created with this special, unique feature. You were created to spring back up. Unbeknownst to you, you had this feature all along, but you only discovered it in the midst of the storm. No one tapped you on the shoulder before the first drop of rain touched down to let you know you'd bounce back. And no one told you how to activate the special feature. It was a gift. It was created to function as an automatic response at exactly the time when needed the most. And the need only came in the midst of the storm.

You may be a mother. You may be a father. Maybe a stepparent or a grandparent. You may relate to the Toy very well from a parent's perspective. Maybe you are a wife. Maybe you are a husband. Maybe you are a friend. Maybe a son or a daughter. Regardless of your role, your title, I'd venture to say you can relate to the Toy on some level, experiencing all the same emotions described before.

And maybe, just maybe, you continue to spring back, hoping that one day, your Maker will come back to see you with a smile on his face, a tear in his eye, and a calming reassurance that He has a plan for you beyond what you can see in the storm. And you persevere, you keep going, because just as you were created with that spring, that special feature, you were also created with a longing for more, with a desire to serve a greater purpose.

Let me bring some good news to you, my friend. The Toy Maker is here. He is often quiet. At times you simply can't hear him, can't see him, because you are surrounded by the raging storm. All you feel is the hail beating down on you; all you hear are the waves crashing against your worn-out body, harder and harder with each passing moment. Your eyes are fixed on what you perceive to be your circumstances.

What if you shift your perception, just ever so slightly, enough to catch sight of the tiny light glimmering off in the distance somewhere? What if you fix your eyes on that light? What if that light begins to grow? What if it grows so big that it becomes all you see? Oh the storm is still raging on, but suddenly your whole world has changed. Your perception has changed.

You clearly see him. The unruly hair. The straggly beard. The shavings of wood chips stuck to his shirt. You see his kind brown eyes; they see right through you. You find yourself breathless. The smells disappear. The unkempt exterior disappears. All you see, all that's left to feel, is the warmth flowing directly from those eyes to your rapidly beating heart until little by little and ever so gently, your heart slows down, your body relaxes, and his eyes squint till they almost disappear. The Toy Maker smiles and nods. You've been given a special feature—a new perception.

Part II

PERCEPTION

4

WARNING: THIS IS GOING TO HURT

Prepare For a Beat-Down

Time to get real. Time to enter the ring. Are you prepared for this? This may be unpleasant. But if you are willing to work hard, and take a bit of a beating, we may just win this thing.

What 'thing,' you ask? I'm talking about overcoming the power that just one little word—*perception*—has over you.

Let us first identify exactly what perception is. According to the dictionary perception is "the act or faculty of perceiving, or apprehending by means of the senses or of the mind."

This would lead us to understand that perception is not based on fact, but rather on a conjuring of thoughts and influences derived from our minds.

What you are aware of you can control.
What you are not aware of controls you.

What you are aware of you can control. What you are not aware of controls you. This concept is based on the idea that in order to control our thinking we must first transfer what is stuck in our unconscious mind to our conscious mind. In other words, we must become aware. Awareness is the first step toward overcoming what we perceive to be true of ourselves.

Reflecting on my own past, I can clearly recall a day that confirmed a perception that had already taken shape in my own mind.

It was a cold, bone-chilling winter afternoon—my birthday to be exact. A cause for celebration. I had just turned 19, a full life ahead of me, the world at my fingertips. Sounds real nice, right? But not exactly how things had gone so far. This birthday, as I dared to look down, head slightly turned to the side as if scared to look, I received a very different birthday surprise.

Positive.

The test result was loud and clear, as if it were *literally* screaming at me. *Positive!*

Years later, I can still remember the sensation that rushed through my body that December day. Overwhelmed, I fell to the bathroom floor, sobbing like a baby. Disbelief, anger, desperation, fear, panic, shame—these and other emotions hitting me as if someone had opened wide that bathroom window and allowed the snowstorm raging outside right into my soul.

"NO! Please, NO!" I screamed out loud as if somehow my screaming would wake me up, as if it were just a dream, a very bad dream. I was pregnant—*again!*

Oh how I loathed those 'other' teenagers, the kids that were once my friends—not a care in the world, endless opportunities—and no *one*, no *thing*, to hold them back from doing anything their heart desires.

As I lay there soaked in tears, I picked my head up to hear my son crying in the other room. There I was, barely 19 years old with a baby from a pregnancy only a little over a year earlier, and now this—*another* child in just a few months. I was overwhelmed.

I managed to pick myself up and wipe my face as I entered my son's room. Picking him up, I held him as I'd never held him before. I loved this child. I lived for this child. He needed me. He was bound to me. And somehow he had this power inside his tiny little body that instantly calmed my soul as I held him, feeling his tiny heart beating against mine.

That day and over the next several months, as I began to come to grips with the fact that my world was about to get even tougher, what I felt was confirmation.

Confirmation: *Yes, I was a disappointment. Yes, I was an embarrassment. Yes, I was a screw-up.*

Confirmation: *No, no one would ever want me. No, I wasn't going to be anything I had hoped for. No, I wasn't worth anything to anyone. No, I wasn't capable of being a good mom, or good at much of anything for that matter.*

I think that up until that day, deep down I was still harboring hope. Yes, I knew I had already messed up—pretty badly, I might add. I already had one unplanned pregnancy behind me. I had experienced more disappointment, more trauma in those nineteen years than many have in a lifetime. Somehow, though, I still held onto hope. But my hope rested in the approval of other people, mainly my own mother. I desperately wanted her to perceive me in a way I hoped I could one day believe to be true.

I once heard someone say, "You can never make a mistake twice because the second time, it's not a mistake. It's a choice." Those words haunted me that day.

This was 'mistake' number two. This baby, this pregnancy. But why stop there? At this point in my life, I felt so much shame and guilt that I don't believe any sense of hope could have transformed my own perception of myself.

I had a long road ahead of me.

What about you? What words would describe how you perceive yourself? But wait, before you answer this question, let's take a look at another man's life and maybe gain a bit more clarity on the significant importance of this question.

Remember the story of Jacob? If you're not familiar, you can find his story in the book of Genesis. Let me refresh your memory.

In simple terms, it's safe to say Jacob came from a pretty dysfunctional family. Maybe you can relate if you have siblings, but Jacob's mom had a favorite son. Jacob's dad had a favorite son. And we see that as the story unfolds, much of Jacob's poor decisions early in his life came from the influence of his mother, who seems to be forever scheming to place her favorite, Jacob, in the forefront. It's worth reading, if you never have (Gen. 25:19-34).

I find that the story of Jacob demonstrates the power of perception rather clearly. Early in the story, you get a clear description of Jacob and his brother Esau. Moses, the author of Genesis, points out the differences between the two brothers. Esau was loved by his father. We get a picture that he was a large 'manly' man. A hunter. A tough, don't-mess-with-me, redneck kind of guy. Jacob, on the other hand, loved by his mother, was quite the opposite. He is described as a quiet fellow. I'd venture to say even a bit of a mama's boy. Holding on to those apron strings rather tightly while mom didn't seem to mind in the least. So much so that she was able to convince Jacob to deceive his own father, her husband, to steal what was rightfully Esau's.

Interesting how there is a subtle implication that Jacob was very aware of what he was *not*. He was *not* like his brother. He was *not* big and strong. He was *not* entitled to the birthright as his brother was. He was *not* his father's favorite. Heck, his father didn't even recognize him as being Jacob when the great deception took place. Jacob may very well had *not* even existed in his father's eyes.

Jacob wanted the blessing from his father, sure. But I'd imagine that Jacob really wanted more than a silly inheritance—an inheritance which seemed to be of more importance to Jacob's mother than to him. I think what Jacob wanted more than anything in the world was his father's acceptance. He wanted to know, to hear, to feel that his father perceived him in such a way that was equal to how he perceived Esau.

He really longed to be valued. To believe his father saw purpose in him.

Those three children in the orphanage, what did they really want? They couldn't have cared less about a silly toy. They wanted what the other children seemed to have been given from the Toy Maker. Something the other children didn't even have the ability to recognize or to appreciate. They couldn't quite pinpoint it, no. But they knew there was something deeper. And they wanted it.

This same question, this same longing, burns deep within all of us. It prods at us, it nags us. Who am I? And what am I meant to become? What is my purpose?

Many of us, myself included, have gone to great extremes to find the answers. We've been impulsive. We've made irrational decisions. We've even gone so far as to deceive, much like Jacob did. If you haven't experienced answers to these questions, it's likely you will continue down some very regrettable paths in hopes of finding the answers, forever searching.

When we burn to know the answers so badly that we're willing to deceive, we'll play dress-up, just as Jacob did. We'll even find helpers in our quest to fake it. With his mother's help, he covered himself in animal skin, throwing on some of Esau's 'manly' smelling clothes, and perhaps lowered his voice a bit to sound more like his father's beloved, his brother Esau.

We pretend. We disguise ourselves to be something we aren't. We appear strong. We appear brave. We appear tough.

We appear intelligent. We appear happy. We laugh at things we don't really find funny. We go to places we don't feel comfortable going to. We do things we know better than to do. Why? Because we fear someone might see us for who we really believe we are, or like Jacob, who we believe we are *not*.

On more than one occasion, I remember getting a surprised reaction from others after I have shared a piece of my story. "Wow, I would have never imagined you'd been through all that," people would say. After sharing my story with one man, I recall him explaining how he was hesitant to meet with me. He had shared quite a bit of his story, his painful past, with me. After he finished, I shared my past struggles with him in return. He said, "I pictured you as one of those 'white-picket-fence' girls. Ya know, the kind of person who has it all, who's never been through anything difficult in their life." He was shocked, to say the least, at all that I revealed that day.

I went home, feeling pretty good about myself. *Huh, I guess I look pretty good on the outside.* Have I finally attained this 'perception' I've been after? Made me kind of sit back and wonder, is this a good thing? Does it simply mean I've overcome so much and I've healed? Or, does it reveal something deeper? Have I learned to ignore those questions still burning in my soul, longing to be answered?

Does this sound familiar?

What about you? Maybe for you, you've actually detached yourself. You've become numb. You're in denial. You never got the approval. You never got an answer to the questions "who am I?" and "what am I to become?"

For many years of my childhood as well as my adult life, this was me. I longed and longed, but each time I searched to get the approval I desperately needed—from whomever or wherever—I just never got it. And so, I became numb. I developed an "I don't need anyone" attitude.

Some of us may look really strong. Tough. But the reality is, we are all about to fall to pieces.

You may have been living your whole life this way. You work harder. You get tougher. But eventually, you get desperate. Desperate trying to get someone else to perceive us differently than we perceive ourselves. We need the approval. But eventually, someone starts to see through us. And they say, "Hey, you don't look so good; what's really going on?"

What if your blessings are just on the other side of your honesty?

Who or what do you look to in order to get these answers?

What answer have you gotten? What labels do you wear?

What would change in you if you didn't have to fake it anymore?

What if what we wished were true of us was actually true?

What if God was waiting on you to be honest? Honest with yourself. Honest with Him. What if your blessings are just on the other side of your honesty?

Are you ready to enter the ring? Are you ready for it to hurt a little ... or a lot? If you long for a more than mediocre life, your answer has to be yes. You are going to need to become vulnerable.

Remember

THERE IS HOPE IN YOUR BROKENNESS

YOU HAVE A **CHOICE**;
YOU **ALWAYS** HAVE A CHOICE

Choose to find **FREEDOM** *in your honesty.*

A TRIP DOWN MEMORY LANE

Let's Camp Out in the Past

John C. Maxwell, a #1 New York Times best-selling author, coach and speaker, was identified as the #1 leader in business by the AMA and the world's most influential leadership expert by Inc. in 2014. His organizations—The John Maxwell Company, The John Maxwell Team, EQUIP, and The John Maxwell Leadership Foundation—have trained over 5 million leaders in every nation.

I share this with you because this man has been an integral part of my growth journey, specifically over the last few years. I've had the honor of meeting with him, and can proudly say he has not only become my mentor, but as he would often say with a huge smile on his face, he is my "friend." I joined what started out as a small group of other hungry people, becoming part of The John Maxwell Team, with aspirations of influencing others to become more than what they ever imagined possible. This team is now growing probably even more than John himself had ever imagined.

"People don't care how much you know until they know how much you care." - John C. Maxwell

Maxwell says, "People don't care how much you know until they know how much you care."

I could share with you all that I 'know,' all that I've learned. But I want more than that for you. I want you to know that I care. I want you to know that when I decided to write this book, to open my life up to hundreds, possibly thousands of complete strangers, it had been with the desire to touch even only one single person. I hope that person is you.

I have much to share with you. If my hope is for you to know I care, that I care about you, there is no getting around this chapter. There is no skipping this part of the book.

I will be authentic. And authenticity requires a certain measure of vulnerability, transparency, and integrity.

Allow me to first set the stage with one of my life's greatest influencers: a beautiful, smart, popular young girl. I wish I could tell you her name, but I cannot. She was a senior in my high school. I had recently transferred there from an inner-city school. A school where I drew no special attention being pregnant. Seemed like every third girl was pregnant. No big deal. But here, in this school, I was alone. There was no one like me. The kids were cruel, much like they still are in school today. No one bothered to whisper as they openly judged me. No being discreet as they looked at me with disgust.

I walked from class to class every day, wishing I was deaf; wishing I couldn't hear the jokes, the laughter; wishing I couldn't see the looks of disgust, or even worse, the ones who ignored me entirely, as if I weren't even there.

But this girl sat with me every single day I had study hall. She'd come in with her friends, and despite their eye-rolls and dismissive looks, she would walk over to where I was sitting. I'd like to say I saved a seat for her, but let's face it—I always had seats open near me. Some days she would talk to me, ask me if I had picked out names for my baby. I had a slew of girl names picked out. Mia was what I had decided on. Some days she would just quietly sit next to me and do homework. She never pitied me, she never apologized for her friends' behavior or crude comments. She simply treated me as 'normal,' like I was no different from the rest of the kids in the school. It was as if all the scary reality of my world would disappear for 45 minutes, and I was normal. I had a friend.

While this may seem insignificant, especially as you read on to discover more of my story, I feel this girl may very well be one of the most influential people in my life. Why, you ask? Because of exactly what my friend John Maxwell stated. "People don't care how much you know until they know how much you care." I don't even remember this girl's name. I don't know much of anything about her, other than she was popular and pretty and took a lot of crap for sitting with me. But I knew how much she cared. And that, all by itself, has had an impact on my entire life, far more than I would have ever dreamed at the time.

Tuck this girl away in the back of your mind. I'll come back to her later.

"When I was a child, I spoke as a child, I understood as a child, I thought as a child. But when I [grew up], I put away childish things.
—1 Corinthians 13:11

Think back to your childhood. Maybe you were in preschool when you were first asked the question, "What do you want to be when you grow up?" Reminiscing on my own answer makes me smile. I wanted to be a princess. But not just any princess. I wanted to be an 'ice-skating princess.' It was during the 1984 Winter Olympics when I first decided that's exactly what I was going to be. Just six years old, wide-eyed, I remember watching in complete amazement as the figure skaters seemed to fly through the air. Such grace, such beauty. I was in complete awe. I wanted nothing more than to be a skating princess.

What about you? Did you want to be a doctor? A firefighter? A ballerina? Do you remember feeling so excited, so full of confidence? It was never a question of, "I wonder if I could be," but rather you KNEW it, as if someone simply asking the question sealed your destiny—"I *will* be."

I, for one, never became an Olympic figure skater. In fact, I seem to remember holding onto the wall for dear life. It's likely you can say the same. You may have become a doctor, but it's not as glamorous as you once thought, is it? You may have become a firefighter, but your dream of becoming a hero isn't exactly how you had envisioned it. Or, you're like the majority of us. You aren't even anywhere near the vicinity of what that innocent childhood dream looked like. There is no magical castle. There is no red cape draped around your shoulders.

What has happened to our dreams since then?

Could it be that we were actually born with a desire for more? It may have started out as a childhood fantasy of becoming a princess or a red-caped hero. But as we grew older, our surroundings, our environment, began to slowly siphon away our dreams. Why? Well, we grew up. We "put away childish things." While we may now look back at those dreams and smile, thinking, "how cute, I thought I'd be a princess," we stop dreaming childish dreams. We stop wishing upon a star.

I'd venture to say that if you looked deep enough within you, it's likely you'll discover that you're still holding on to a version of your childhood fantasy. It may have morphed into something a bit different. But nonetheless, it's still there, just buried beneath your perception of your current reality.

Amber Noelle

Where did you come from?

In the story The Toy Maker, the three children saw themselves as orphans. There is a clear implication that they never left one another's side. They were bound together. And yet, something was missing. As young children, they weren't aware of it. They were happy, content. They viewed their surroundings as 'normal.' It wasn't until they were presented with something more that they realized there was something missing. Their perception began to shift. The reality of their environment had not changed, yet they experienced it differently than they once had.

I grew up in a small town in Pennsylvania. I was the youngest of three children. I had a sister who was three years older than I, and a brother, ten years my senior. I had a mom. I had a dad. We lived in a comfortable house. My sister and I shared a bedroom while my brother inherited the entire finished basement—not fair, I know! Pretty normal sibling stuff in my house. My sister and I shared a bunk bed. I can remember several nights when I'd run out of my room to 'tell' on my sister. Every night, I would insist that she had to 'watch over me' from above in her top bunk until I fell asleep. Usually she would agree, just to shut me up, I'm sure. But once in a while she would refuse and I'd go running.

I can remember waking up in the middle of the night, having had a bad dream. I can recall running to my mother's bedroom a few times, and how she'd yell at me for waking her up and tell me to go back to bed. Typically, I'd go straight to my father's room. I'd crawl into his twin size bed and insist that he stay awake until I fell asleep. He'd wrap his arm around me, and within seconds, he was snoring again. But I was safe. He had me wrapped snugly, and I knew I was okay.

This is where you pause and re-read that last paragraph. Yes, that is correct. While my sister and I were crammed into one room in our three-bedroom house, my parents each had their own separate bedroom. This was normal to me. I didn't know any different. Bear with me as I paint a picture of what exactly 'normal' looked like for me in my home.

My 'Normal'

Normal meant ... Mom and Dad never touched. I don't recall ever hearing an 'I love you' being shared between the two of them. I don't even recall a hug or a kiss being exchanged.

Normal meant ... Mom and Dad didn't talk. Once in a while, after my sister and I were in bed, I'd hear the pastor come over to the house and I'd overhear my mom crying or yelling at someone. I assumed she was yelling at my dad.

Normal meant ... Many nights, I'd hear the front door open and close. I'd get up, go look for my dad, but he wasn't home. His car was there in the driveway, but he was not home. I can recall waiting to hear the door open again. Sometimes it did before I drifted back to sleep. Most times though, I'd ask him in the morning, "Dad, where did you go last night?" He'd explain he just went for a walk. I remember scolding him, firmly explaining what my expectations were from him. He was not to leave the house without telling me where he was going, or that he'd be back. Dad just put one arm around me, and with a sweet smile, said he was sorry and that I was not to worry.

Normal meant ... Dad went to work during the day. Came home to a home-cooked meal by my mother, who was nothing short of a magician in the kitchen. After dinner, my dad would retreat to the garage. What was once a two-car garage had been converted into my dad's 'workshop.' He spent most of his time in that workshop. And almost every waking moment of my existence was spent there with him. He worked at his drafting table while I sat at his desk, drawing pictures. I was glued to my dad. Wherever he was, I was there. Whatever he was doing, I wanted to do it too.

Normal meant ... We would go to church every weekend. Usually, my mom and dad would drive separately. And every Friday night, we would gather in the living room to have 'worship.' We'd have our weekly Friday night meal—fruit salad and popcorn. And my mom would read a chapter or two from one of the Bible story books we had, or we'd listen to a story on a cassette tape.

I loved Friday nights. Somehow, it felt really good and really warm, lying on the floor with my sister, staring up at the ceiling while half-listening to my mom read, half-zoning out from wondering what it would be like if the room were upside-down and we lived on the ceiling. Weird kid, I know.

What does your 'normal' look like?

This odd question is a whole lot more important than you might think. Your view of normal is what shaped your perception. Don't skip over this question. Ask it. Answer it. Honestly.

Remember

THERE IS HOPE IN YOUR BROKENNESS

YOU HAVE A CHOICE;
YOU ALWAYS HAVE A CHOICE

Choose to find **FREEDOM** *in your honesty.*

6

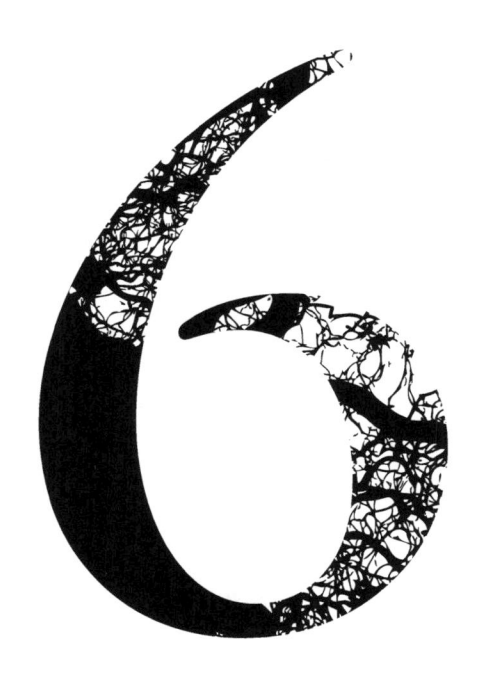

A LITTLE
FURTHER NOW

Go Within—or Go Without

Sometimes when you're in a dark place, you think you've been buried, but actually, you've been planted. We always have a choice, right? This is how I will choose to view the story I'm about to share with you. That there was purpose in my past. That there *is still* purpose in my past. And furthermore, let me boldly say, there is purpose in *your* past. But we must be willing to go within to begin to uncover what that might be.

I remember deciding I wanted to live with Dad. My parents were splitting up and the choice was given to me: live with Dad or live with Mom.

I had been known to stick like glue to my dad. Day in and day out, I followed him around like a puppy. I'd walk out to the end of the driveway every morning to watch him drive away down the long road until I couldn't see his car anymore. I'd anxiously wait for him to get home from work every day. I laugh as I remember one day thinking I'd really impress him and 'cut the grass' for him. He'd be so proud of me. I found a pair of scissors and proceeded to cut the entire lawn for him. I may have sat there in the grass for half an hour, snipping away, before I realized this was nuts!

The simple fact was, I adored my dad. He was the one I snuggled with, tucked under his arm while he read the newspaper or worked on a crossword puzzle. He was the one I took long walks with, holding his hand all the way. He was the one I spent countless hours with in his workshop. There weren't ever many words shared between us, just a quiet sense of belonging. I belonged to him. I felt warm and safe and at peace in his presence.

So there wasn't much to my decision. It was an easy one.

Or was it? Not sure exactly what changed my mind. Maybe the fact that my mom was moving out—out of our house, out of our small quiet town. Maybe I was excited at the thought of something new, something different. But for whatever reason I can't quite recall, I changed my mind. And within a few months, I was packing up, leaving the familiarity of my home, off to embark on a new adventure.

My sister was just leaving to attend a local Christian boarding school. My brother had left the house a few years prior. So it was just me and my mom. I recall my sister always having the caliber of relationship with my mom that I seemed to have with my dad. They goofed around a lot—always laughing at something while I thought they were just being stupid, never really found what was so funny. I didn't have that same kind of bond with my mom as my sister did. But nonetheless, I chose her.

We moved several times over the next few years. Our first 'home' was the top two floors of an old house. There was a little old lady who lived on the first floor. Mrs. Potts. You had to walk through her front door and through her house to get to our little nook we called home.

I was about 11 years old when we lived with her. I remember getting off the bus and smelling the cookies she had baked as she greeted me at the door. Big smile on her face, cookies in hand, five days a week, like clockwork. My mom didn't know this woman prior to living there. She just answered the ad in the paper, inquiring about the vacant apartment upstairs. But every day, Mrs. Potts lured me over to her couch and asked about my day. One might think this woman had nothing better to do than bake cookies for some kid she hardly knew. I loved this part of my day. And yes, those cookies were to die for. But there was something else about Mrs. Potts that stirred anticipation in me as the bus grew closer to the house every day. The same anticipation I remembered while waiting for my dad to drive home down that long road, back into our driveway.

My mom worked a lot. She was an intake coordinator for a drug and alcohol referral service in the city. Some days she came home straight after work. Other days, she came home much later. My sister was gone. So the usual goofiness and laughter I'd heard around my mom went silent. My sister seemed to have a way of bringing out the best in her. I, on the other hand, never connected with Mom in the same way. I'd wash the dishes, or tidy up the house, anything to try to connect with her in some way. But most days, when she did come home, she didn't talk much. She was tired and sad most of the time. She withdrew. I withdrew.

After only a few months living there, Mrs. Potts died. She had cancer. I hadn't known it at the time. I didn't know she was dying. Maybe had I known, I would have baked cookies for her one day. I remember feeling so sad. And odd as it may sound, I was angry at my mom when Mrs. Potts died. Why was my mom sad about it when I was the one who spent every afternoon with the dear sweet old lady? I was all she had. Mrs. Potts cared enough about *me* to ask me how my day was. I had the right to be sad. I had grown to love her, and I knew she loved me back.

Thinking back now, I have to wonder, did she know she was dying? It was likely she did. And if so, why did she choose to spend her last days baking cookies for some chubby kid who clearly didn't need any more cookies? And why me? She hardly knew me. The question still burns in my mind. I have to wonder if she, like the Toy Maker, saw something in me, something that needed more. And for the last few days of her life, she was bound and determined to fill me up with more than just warm, freshly baked cookies.

This is when I can recall first feeling resentment toward my mom. Somehow, in my mind, it was her fault Mrs. Potts died.

Someone saw something in me. I didn't know what it was. I only knew it was 'more.'

So much more died that fall than just an old woman I hardly knew. It was a sense of value, of worth, of purpose. Someone saw something in me. I didn't know what it was. I only knew it was *more*.

Again, I packed up my room. Off to a new apartment. Only a few miles down the road, but this place was much smaller. Just a two-bedroom apartment. No sweet old lady downstairs; rather, a whole building full of strangers, each living in their own tiny space.

I remember the day Mom brought Sam home. He was a very large man. A black man. I didn't even think my parents knew any 'black' people. I remember him being very quiet. He was intimidating to look at, towering above me at probably well over six feet. But he was the sweetest man—very quiet, very kind to me. I wasn't really sure why he was there or how my mom even knew him. But he'd come over for dinner. And oftentimes when I woke up in the morning, he was still there. Call me naive, but I didn't really get it. He wasn't around for very long. But there was usually another man quickly to follow.

My mom had taken a second job, and I soon learned where these men had come from. Many evenings she'd come home from her day job, pick me up, and we'd head into the city where she worked her second job. Again, wasn't quite sure where I was, and sometimes it felt a little uncomfortable being the only kid there. But I remember a familiar feeling. The same feeling I had with my dad. The same feeling I had with Mrs. Potts.

I'd sit in the 'lounge' area with the other adults. I remember thinking that some of them were not looking so good—not real clean, kind of distraught-looking. But there were always one or two women or men who would sit next to me on the couch and just talk. Or better yet, listen. I had grown to be quite the talker. Anyone who was willing to listen to me surely got more than they bargained for. To this day, my dad still has a magnet holding my picture up on his refrigerator saying, "Help, I'm talking and I can't shut up!"

As men came and went from our apartment, I recognized them from the rehab. The same lounge area where I'd sit and make conversation in the evenings, waiting for time to pass, was the same lounge area where these men usually came from. There were nights in that small apartment—the head of my bed only inches away from the wall that separates mine and my mother's room—that I had wished I were deaf. I wished I could just go to sleep and pretend I was anywhere but there. Maybe back in Mrs. Potts' living room, eating cookies on her couch.

I became more of a nuisance, more of a responsibility, a burden even. So for the most part, I just kept to myself. I stayed out of her way. And Mom didn't seem to mind the space.

This pattern went on for a few years. By then, we had moved a few more times. We seemed to have an unspoken agreement of sorts: I stay out of her way, she stays out of mine. I found myself craving excitement. Anything to take me outside of my home, anything to get some kind of interaction—*any* kind of interaction.

By the time Thaddeus first walked through the door, I had gotten pretty used to new faces. Didn't really faze me; I was rarely in the house. After school, if I didn't skip, I'd come home, and within a half hour I was out the door. Center city was only about two miles away—up a few hills, across the 8th Street bridge. That's where I made myself at home. That's where I felt alive. That's where I got attention.

To see me or know me now, you'd likely laugh in my face. *Tough bad-ass* is anything *but* what you'd describe me as. As the man I referenced earlier described, a 'white-picket-fence kind of girl.' But that wasn't at all what I was after. That's exactly what I aimed to destroy. That white-picket-fence girl felt too much pain. I'd rather not be her.

Thaddeus was similar to the other men. I knew he had served time in prison and had recently been released. Didn't know what for, didn't really care. He was a bit younger than the others, maybe in his thirties, hard to say. Nice enough, I guess. He seemed to be a bit of a bad-ass, and I thought that was pretty cool.

Over the next few months, he spent a lot of time with me. He didn't work, at least not a 'regular' job, so he was around a lot. He proved to be very different from the other men in more ways than one. I liked him. He told me nice things. Complimented me. Showed interest in things that I was interested in. He reassured me that he cared about me, and for the first time in a long time, I actually *felt* it. Someone did care about me.

At this point, my mom and I were at each other's throat day and night. I was barely around. She had absolutely no idea what I was doing or who I was hanging out with. And while she partially seemed relieved to have me out of her hair, she sure took the time to make crazy accusations. She called me a 'druggie,' accused me of dealing. She made fun of how I dressed. I wish

I had a dollar for every time I heard her say, "Pull your damn pants up!" Who cares anyway. I was free. Doing whatever I wanted; who cares what she thought.

But Thaddeus cared. He started to back me up whenever my mom and I argued. And sure enough, within a few weeks, with his arm around my shoulders, he said to me with compassion, "I'm sorry your mom doesn't really care about you. I'm sorry you have nobody." Then with a firm reassurance, "But I do. I love you. I care about you."

It felt good. At first. After a few more weeks, what started as an arm around the shoulders turned into his hands on my waist, and then later, holding me on the couch after my mom had gone to bed.

By this time, I believed—no, I *perceived*—that no one loved me. No one cared. No one, that is, except him. I didn't particularly like how he touched me. But by the same token, at least someone cared enough to think I was pretty, to think I was attractive. I was no cute girl back then. I was chubby and did my best to look the part of 'inner-city-bad-ass-don't-mess-with-me-kid.' Then one day, he decided to 'take me away from it all,' as he had been promising me for months. Maybe it would be easier to explain it as a kidnapping, but the truth was, he told my mom he was taking me on 'vacation,' and she didn't really care.

As I got into his cousin's car, something deep inside me felt uneasy that day. Uneasy would be putting it lightly. I felt downright scared. But this tough girl wasn't going to let any fear get the best of me. We drove for hours, down to West Virginia, somewhere deep in the woods. I had no clue where I was. It was like nothing I had ever seen before. We drove down a dirt road through the woods until we arrived. There were mobile homes kind of just parked any which way. No rhyme or reason to it. They looked as if they were ready to collapse at any moment.

There were women walking around, half-dressed, skinny, sick-looking, and almost in a daze it seemed. And there were men. Lots of them. Some of them looked similar to the women I saw. Some were old, some young.

We got out of the car. We walked to the first mobile home. An old man answered the door. I was told to go in the other room and watch TV while I overheard them arguing. They were arguing about me. I'm not sure what about, but when he grabbed my hand and stormed out of there, I couldn't help but see the man looking down at me. He looked at me as if he wore on his face every ounce of pain I had ever felt. He had tears in his eyes. And I had a bad feeling in my heart.

Now holding my hand a bit firmer than usual, Thaddeus and I walked from one mobile home to the next. To some people, he introduced me as his daughter, receiving a look of disbelief. Me, being as white as white gets. Him, being as black as black gets. No way I'm his daughter. But most times, he introduced me as his 'girl' or his 'girlfriend.' Within an hour of arriving, he led me to a shed. He brought me inside and firmly explained that he had things to do and I was to stay there.

By this time, I wasn't hearing his kind voice reassuring me that he loved me, that he cared about me. His entire tone had changed. He ordered me to stay there and not dare try to leave. There was no bathroom. It was only a small metal shed, enough room to maybe fit a riding mower. I stayed there, curled up on a cot, for what felt like weeks. It was likely just a few days, but who really knows. He would come in from time to time and give me food, let me pee outside, and then come back inside with me. He touched me in ways much different from what he had done in my house. He was suddenly much more aggressive and forceful.

There are moments of that experience I only remember in very vague detail. There are other moments where I can recall a distinct sound, a distinct smell, and the distinct feeling of pure panic and fear. It was one of the first times in my life I vividly remember praying in sheer desperation. My gut was telling me I wasn't going to live past my 13 years of life. I begged him to let me go home. "Please just take me home. I won't tell anybody, I promise. I just wanna go home, please."

And God came through for me that week. The monster who had once been someone I thought to have loved me brought me home. He dropped me off a few blocks from my house, and vanished, never to be seen again. I ran home as fast as I could. I remember practically breaking down the front door as I ran inside and locked the door. I was hysterical. Crying so hard. Hyperventilating. I could barely talk. My mom was getting angrier by the minute, demanding to know what happened and where her boyfriend was.

An hour or so later I was in the hospital. After a few days there, I was allowed visitors. My mom came to see me. I assumed she had been informed by the hospital staff about all that had happened to me. I was looking forward to seeing her. See, I loved my mom, I always did. And all I wanted that day was to see my mom walk in the door, wrap me in her arms, and tell me how much she loved me and that everything was going to be okay, everything was going to change. When she walked through the door that day, she had tears in her eyes. *Yes*, I thought, *she loves me. She's going to tell me all I've been needing to hear.*

She sat next to my bed and leaned in close, her eyes welling up with tears. And in a quiet voice laced with more disappointment than I had ever heard in someone's voice, said, "Amber, how am I ever supposed to have a boyfriend if you're going to take them away from me?"

I'd love to end this chapter right now. I'd like to transition to a 'happily ever after.' And let me reassure you, just in case you're ready to put this book down, there *is* more. There *is* a happily ever after. I'll get there, just hang with me for a few more pages.

"May I never forget that on my best day I need God as desperately as I did on my worst day."

I can't clearly pinpoint what I would describe as 'my worst day.' There were so many 'worse days' to follow after I was released from the hospital that summer.

Things got increasingly miserable in my mom's house. We screamed at each other relentlessly. And there weren't any more boyfriends for a while. By the end of that summer, my parents decided to send me off to the Christian boarding school where my sister was still attending, going into her senior year.

I spent two years there. During the first year, my sister, although well-intended, tried to steer me back onto a straight path. I wanted nothing to do with her and her lecturing. Deep down, although my abuser had left, I still believed what he told me, that no one really loved me. No one really cared. My mom seemed to reaffirm that on a daily basis. And clearly, my sister was just trying to control my life. What did she know, anyway? She had the kind of relationship with my mom that I never had.

When I think back on it now, my heart breaks to know how much my sister loved me then, and how much her own heart must have been breaking at not being able to help her little sister.

No one seemed to understand me there. I didn't really talk about what happened. I didn't really know *how* to talk about it, what to say, how to explain it to anyone. I already felt that no one liked me, so no need going about and making myself look like a freak.

So I got tougher. The walls got taller. This girl got 'badder.'

> Meanwhile, the worthlessness got bigger.
> The shame got thicker.
> The guilt became more powerful.
> The anger got meaner.
> The resentment got deeper.
> The depression became more severe.
> The pain got scarier.
> The voices got louder.
> The anxiety became unmanageable.

After spending two years in the boarding school, having gotten into my fair share of trouble there, I blew out my knee. *Praise God*, I thought. *A reason to get out of this place.* Although I believed in God and all that 'stuff,' I never really experienced Him for myself. I mean, let's be real here—He didn't seem to be too concerned with me and what I wanted. That was my perception.

So I headed back home to Mom's house once again, had ACL surgery, and spent the next summer at home, working two jobs. Carvel Ice Cream and Dunkin' Donuts. Can you say "chubby?" It's safe to say I wasn't doing my already-thick waistline any favors by working three months hopping from eating muffins and donuts all night to ice cream all day. By the end of that summer, I had saved up enough money to buy my first junker car, a 1988 Ford Escort. Man, was I proud of this car. It felt amazing to have worked so hard for something and have it all be mine.

But to me, this car meant more than a sense of pride for having earned it. It meant that I no longer had to walk a few miles into the city. I could drive there now. And what was more, I might even make some new friends.

And make new friends is exactly what I did. I had just turned 16 that last December and after working all summer, saving every penny for this pride and joy some simply call a 'car,' I was ready to take on the world—me, the chubby little 5-foot-2-inch little bad-ass that I was (or more accurately, *wasn't*). I met a lot of people over the first few months I had that car. One was a guy I had often seen around while hanging out on the street. Don't ask me his name, I have no clue. All I know is that he whistled at me a few times, gave me one of those "Damn girl, you look good" kind of 'compliments,' and I was hooked. That's right, it didn't take much. For the next couple weeks, I drove this man around, bumping to 'Biggie Smalls' blasting out of my cassette player while he popped in and out of places delivering the 'goods.'

Yes, 16 years old now, big and bad, driving a drug dealer around. Then I got the brilliant idea to drive him all the way up to New York City one weekend. Sure, not a problem, why not? We were in a back alley somewhere. He was taking a really long time, longer than usual. And I panicked. For the first time since I had been in West Virginia, fearing I'd never see my home again or my mom, I panicked. I felt a sudden rush of anxiety and an urgent need to get out of there, and fast. So I left. Yes, that's right. I left. I left this man stranded in New York City and I found my way back home. I spent the next few weeks scared. But nonetheless, I still roamed the streets, looking for the next trouble I could find for myself.

Didn't take long until 'trouble' found me—exactly right, you guessed it, the dealer I had left stranded. And he wasn't happy to see me in the least. He dragged me up into what I assumed was his apartment right there off the street, and proceeded to rape me. Now, thanks to three months of Dunkin' Donuts and Carvel Ice Cream, I wasn't a frail little kid. So I fought. I fought that day as if I were fighting everyone who had let me down. But he was no small man himself. I can still feel my two little hands getting crushed as he squeezed both to pin them over my head, while with his other hand, he started taking my jeans off. I was sure the tiny bones in my fingers were going to snap.

I cried out to God once again, "Save me!" I thought once more that this was the last time I was going to breathe. And all I could remember thinking was: I want my mom.

God came through. The man was big, but God was bigger. He let me go. I flew down those stairs crying hysterically. And once again, I ran straight to my mom. After all, hers was the face I pictured before I thought this man would surely kill me after he raped me.

But I was running right back into the arms of disappointment. "Whatever, Amber, no one's going to believe you. I don't even believe you. All you want is attention."

Needing a Mom ... to Being a Mom

Now 17, I went to an inner-city public school, which was nothing at all like the Christian boarding school I'd gone to two years before. I was used to the rough crowd by now. I gravitated toward them. You should be getting a pretty clear picture of where my sense of value and self-worth were. So it should come as no surprise that the pattern wasn't changing simply because of one bad experience after another. Stubborn kid I was. Stubborn lady I am still, to be completely transparent!

I'll spare you the intimate details this time ... There was a boy. There was a girl. A few months later, this girl was pregnant. *Pregnant.* Interesting how the first thing that popped into my head was not, "Oh crap, I'm 17 and I'm gonna have a baby." No. Instead, it was, "Great! I've got to tell my mom."

By this time, I had come to expect nothing less than a disappointing or sarcastic remark from her. She was constantly accusing me of things, some of which I hadn't even done. Other things, well, I had been doing. No, I wasn't dealing drugs. But I'd been driving a dealer. Does that count? And I'd been doing drugs myself. Does that count? In any event, I prepared myself for maybe the biggest disappointment to date. I was pregnant. So her accusations of me being a 'slut' were going to be justified now in her mind. It went something like this:

"Mom, I have to tell you something."

"Wait, let me guess." With a smirk and a chuckle, she said, "You're pregnant."

Head hanging low, I mumbled, "Yes Mom, I am."

"I figured, Amber, that it was only going to be a matter of time."

Telling my boyfriend would prove to be difficult as well. Being only 17 himself, he was in no way hoping to be a dad. Throughout the next nine months and beyond that, even after my son was born, this boy would hit me. He sat on top of my pregnant belly and choked me until I nearly passed out. He pushed me over couches, down the stairs. You name it. Once in a while he would even raise his hand at me, just to get me to flinch. Then he'd laugh puffing up his chest, knowing I was scared of him.

I left my mom's house and moved in with my boyfriend, his mom and two brothers. His grandparents lived next door. I adored his grandfather. He always seemed to know what was going on and tried to help me. My eldest son carries on his memory through his middle name, Felipe. And I loved his mom. She took me in. Instead of ridiculing me, or shaming me, she seemed excited to be a grandmother. But by the time the school found out I was not living with my mom anymore, I was forced to leave. Either go back to my mom—which wasn't an option because she told me if I leave, I wasn't coming back—or go live with my dad.

So I left. Got through most of my senior year of high school, and then moved out on my own. My dad paid $300 for a third-floor space in the city, and I made it work. After my son was born, it took me only a few months to muster enough courage to leave his dad. Something changed in me. I was bound and determined to be a better mom to this little baby than my mom was to me. I experienced some pretty severe abuse over those last few months. But again, was I really worthy of any better than what I was receiving? No, not really—or so I perceived.

What made the difference, what gave me the courage to leave, was that I now had this little baby boy, staring up at me, crying through the night, and often clinging to me as if he himself were needing what I had been needing. Just a baby, but already taking in so much, already seeming to develop a sense of insecurity, a sense of fear. I wanted better for him. And that was all I chose to focus on.

Before long, as I described in Chapter 4, I was pregnant again. Different dad. Different bad situation. But same disappointment. Same failure of a daughter. Same path, going nowhere good.

Free to Choose, But Never Freed of the Consequences of Your Choice

I was working now. Managed to get an associates' degree at a technical school. With financial help from my dad and babysitting help from him and some wonderful church members, I went to school during the day. Came home in the afternoon and went to work at night. I managed to graduate, even received the Outstanding Student Award in my graduating class. Pretty big deal. Kind of humorous in a way, since I had never considered myself to be outstanding in much of anything—other than screwing up.

I remember graduation day. I remember putting on my gown, thankful that I could cover up my belly, as it was just starting to become obvious that those weren't donuts in there but a baby.

I got a good job right after graduation, working as a Web Designer. I worked a full eight hours, and then many nights. I'd pick up my boys from daycare, feed them, and then head right back to work, oftentimes working right through the night to make ends meet. I'd set up the pack-and-play for my older son while my younger son slept next to me in his carseat. I remember many nights popping caffeine pills just to keep awake, to keep going, and then do it all over again the next day.

My younger son was about eight months old when I met a man. Let's just say this man was different from any boy I had ever been involved with. He had a job. He was white. He had a nice family. He was pretty nice too, and he seemed to like my boys. And what's more, he seemed to like me. All good things, right? All things my mom would approve of. Within a year, we were married.

It was in the first year of my marriage that I realized I made what may have been one of my biggest mistakes to date. But nonetheless, I chose to stay. That first year, we fought often. Deep down, I knew I should leave before it got worse. There were red flags waving all over the place, as if to say, "Amber, get out now!" But I kept looking at my boys. They had a father. I kept looking in the mirror, reminding myself that this man was better than any I had ever had, and in reality, I didn't really deserve better anyway. Heck, in my own warped perception of myself, I didn't even deserve him.

I faced a choice I didn't want to make: leave now and once again slap on an even bigger 'FAILURE' label, or stay and begin to accept that in order to make this marriage work, I was going to have to 'learn my role and shut my hole.' And so I stayed. I learned to 'shut my hole' and I took on the role of a quiet, obedient, submissive wife that was expected of me.

I spent the next 11 years of my life pouring myself into my kids. I was so incredibly happy to have my boys, and now a daughter too. It was all that brought me joy, all that mattered to me. It was okay that I wasn't happy in my marriage. It was okay as long as I could be a mom, and I could be someone who loved and cared for my kids in a way that they deserved.

I could take the time to write three books just describing all that was wrong in my marriage, all I have learned and experienced through it. What I will simply say is this: If you could combine all my experiences prior to my divorce, I would describe them as a spring shower—just enough to need an umbrella and give you a slight chill. Compare that pre-divorce spring shower to a post-divorce tsunami. Not even in the same ballpark. No comparison.

Oftentimes in life, the choices that seem right are often wrong. I had believed that this marriage would prove to be best for my kids, best even for me. But that was not the case ... or was it? There comes that pesky word again—perception. Is it possible that some of our painful past experiences occurred for the sole purpose of altering our perception?

You will either find yourself empowered by all of these painful experiences, or you can feel sorry for yourself, stuck in self-pity.

Remember

THERE IS HOPE IN YOUR BROKENNESS
YOU HAVE A CHOICE;
YOU ALWAYS HAVE A CHOICE

Choose to be REFINED by your past rather than ALLOW it to define you.

7

VALID

You and Your 'Feelings'

I'll never forget these words spoken to me, "Oh here we go again, you and your 'feelings,'" and how this person referred to my feelings as 'psycho-babble.'

I can remember questioning my feelings. Should I not be feeling the way I do? The question itself made me feel angry. *Who are you to mock my feelings*, I thought.

How many of us have grown up hearing from other, oftentimes well-meaning adults that we shouldn't feel bad? Or don't feel sad. Or don't get mad. Don't cry. From a young age, it was instilled in our subconscious that some feelings—not all—but some feelings are 'wrong.' Anger. Resentment. Bitterness. Shame. Guilt. You expend enormous amounts of energy trying to 'not' feel something that your conscious mind is very much telling you to feel.

So what do you do as a result? You suppress those feelings. You ignore them. You hide them. Otherwise, you risk the chance of hearing, "Oh here we go again, you and your feelings."

Validation

Allow me to share some comforting news with you. Your feelings are valid. To clarify: I'm not saying your feelings are a reflection of what's accurate. What I'm saying is that based simply on the fact that you are feeling them means they are valid. Not just some of your feelings, but ALL of your feelings. What's even better news is that, as I shared earlier, not only do you have the power to change your story, you also have the ability to alter your feelings. And sure enough, it all boils down to your perception.

A few years ago, after the Creative Kafe idea quickly retreated to the back burner of my brain, I entered into the personal training business. I received my personal training certification. I poured my heart and soul into building a brand, which I called Muscles and Mascara, Training for Chicks. The whole idea behind the business was to work with women—not only helping them in the area of physical fitness, but to tap into something deeper. I dreamed of inspiring other women, of reaching them on a personal level through training, and to provide them with much more than just a promise of physical transformation.

Funny thing, when you decide to act on an idea, when you decide to act on an inspiration. One thing you can be sure of is that you will face opposition. Guaranteed. And this particular venture was no exception. Once again, I heard from my constant course of ridicule, in an attempt to undermine my value, "Look at you, all 'inspirational.' Meanwhile, you can't even make $10,000 a year."

Truth be told, the business didn't last more than a year before I relocated and had to put the business on the back burner. I didn't make much money. In fact, it cost me far more than $10,000 to even start the business. And when I relocated, I had taken a loss.

The thing is, I wasn't interested in becoming rich. In fact, as crazy as it may sound, I knew deep down that I wasn't going to be in this business for very long. But something (or more accurately *Someone*) told me, "Amber, start this business. Pour everything you've got into it—money, heart, and soul. Use it. Use it as an opportunity to grow. Use it as an opportunity to reach other women." So, based on my intent, I was a success. But based on my wallet, I was a failure. Which one am I to believe?

I chose to hear the words of the man telling me I was a failure because I wasn't making money. I chose to hear the words of the same man telling me my *feelings* weren't valid.

Over and over again, for years now, I've been listening to the wrong man. I've been hearing the voice of my accuser in my head. Ridiculing me. Shaming me. Pointing his finger at me as he laughs at what he perceives to be my failures.

GREAT QUESTIONS TO ASK AND TO ANSWER HONESTLY.

AMBER NOELLE

Who are you listening to? Who is this enemy in your head? Consider now that this voice, although it may sound like the voice of your mom or your dad, your boss, your ex-husband or your ex-wife, your mother-in-law or whomever, it is something bigger than that. And that 'something bigger' is controlling you, whether you like to admit it or not.

Remember when I told you in the beginning of this book that you have the opportunity to rewrite your story? One of the most fundamental steps is simply to accept that your feelings are valid. And not only are they valid, it's okay to feel them.

It's okay to feel angry. It's another story to act out in anger.

It's okay to feel resentment. It's another story to continually remind someone of how they've wronged you.

It's okay to feel sad. It's another story to let that sadness spiral into depression.

Do these 'negative' emotions feel good? No way. Of course not. Feeling like you've let someone down or feeling as if you've failed once again is a far cry from ideal. But what if you knew this could be the last time you feel those feelings, at least to this degree? Would you jump all over that? Sure you would. Of course.

Now what if I told you that you're going to have to allow yourself to feel them first. I'm not talking about feeling them as you do now—where you immediately try to dismiss them, or hide them, or ignore them altogether. I'm asking you to sit on them for a while. If you're angry, sit and stew in your anger. If you're resentful, yell out loud about how you've been wronged.

Feel it. Feel it like you've never felt it before. Choose to feel it on your own terms before you no longer have control over the terms.

Be honest with God. Be real. Don't hold back.

And, if I may, let me take it even one step further. Yell at God. Yes, you read that correctly. Be honest to God with your feelings. We often forget or more likely have never realized, that God wants all of us. He doesn't say, "Come to Me, all you who are 'happy and joyful.'" No, He says, "Come to me, all you who are weary." And furthermore, He says, "I will give you rest." He's not asking for us to get all cleaned up before we come to Him. Nor does He want us to come to Him with only our joys and praises. Be honest with God. Be raw. Be real. Don't hold back.

I remember saying to my three kids on several occasions over the past several years, "Listen, there may be times when you're really mad at me. There may be times that you hate me, that you resent me, that you feel so much anger toward me, you want to explode." Then I'd tell them, "Please do." I wanted them to come to me with anything. Of course, no parent wants their kids to disrespect them, to yell at them, to mistreat them. But, in the midst of their own struggles, in the most difficult times of their lives, I wanted them to be honest. I wanted them to trust me with their true, honest, and raw feelings. I knew it would hurt if they took their feelings out on me and directed their anger at me. But I'd follow up with, "Know that no matter what happens, no matter how you treat me, what you say to me, how you feel about me, I will never stop loving you. And

I will always accept you. And I will always be here when you need me."

This may sound like enabling. And sure enough, I found out there is a very fine line between supportive and enabling behavior. But I didn't want my own children, who I love more than anything in the world, to ever feel that there was nowhere to go when they felt their worst. They needed a 'safe place.' They needed a source to come to—day or night, angry or sad, scared or lost—and know in their little hurting hearts that it truly was safe to come to me no matter what.

If you have your own children, this may really resonate with you. When you open yourself up, even go so far as to welcome this kind of honesty from someone else, you risk a lot. You risk your own feelings being hurt. You risk rejection. You risk loss.

Do you think God wants anything less from us? Don't you think he loves and cares for us more than we do our own children? Would you be willing to sacrifice just a little hurt, rejection, or loss just so your kids would be 'okay'? Sure. Most of us would say yes. But would you be willing to sacrifice one of them to try to reach some stranger, or even worse, someone who hates you, someone who you feel that same hatred for in return? Someone in which there is absolutely no guarantee that they will be receptive to your help? No. Of course not. But God did. God said, "I'll send My Son—My only Son. I know He's going to suffer. Suffer at the hands of the very ones I send Him there for. I know He's going to carry the pain and suffering of every single soul there now and yet to come."

Don't you think God wants our honesty? Decide right now, before you read any further, that you are going to commit to being honest with God. You will be honest with yourself. You will accept your feelings—no matter what they are—as valid.

For you, what are those feelings? What is your immediate, impulsive reaction to a situation or experience? Is it anger? Defensiveness? Or do you hang your head and feel shame or guilt? Maybe it varies depending on the particular circumstance. Take another trip down memory lane with me. Think back to your reactions as a child. It may surprise you just how little you've changed since then.

In thinking back to my own childhood, I can distinctly remember repeatedly saying, "I'm sorry." It didn't matter what the situation was, didn't matter if I was actually at fault for something, or if I actually made a mistake. If there was any discomfort being felt by someone else, my reaction would always be to take responsibility for anyone else's discomfort. Then when I was reminded to stop saying I'm sorry, I'd quickly respond with, "I'm sorry."

First Impressions

I think I was just 7 or 8 years old when I first started writing. I illustrated and wrote my first 'book.'

We were visiting my grandparents. I can still remember the aroma that day and how stuffed my belly felt after gorging myself on my grandmother's Thanksgiving dinner. I can even remember what I was wearing. The adults were gathered around the dinner table, drinking coffee, picking at the last bits of dessert. My sister and I were sitting on my grandmother's couch, bored out of our minds. She got herself comfortable on one end of the couch while I curled up on the other end. She was drifting off to sleep. I, on the other hand, was wide awake with nothing to do. I got up and dug around in my grandfather's filing cabinet where we'd usually find his hidden stash of black licorice.

Grabbing a handful while he wasn't watching, my eye caught a glimpse of a blank notebook. I asked my grandfather if I could have it. He was sipping, or more accurately, chewing on some warm milk, which always seemed odd to me, but he just waved his hand as if to brush me off.

So I dug around for some colored pencils and sat down to get to work.

I left the front cover blank. Figured I'd think of a catchy title after I finished writing the book. It started out with drawings of bunny rabbits and squirrels scampering around in the snow. I remember describing the town in which these furry creatures lived. It was Christmastime, and the town was excited as ever. I drew pictures of my family. And as the story progressed, I drew a picture of a little girl named Amber.

She had just gone to bed after spending the day unwrapping gifts and playing with toys. She just loved the Christmas season. So as Amber went to bed that night, a fairy came to visit her. She told the fairy, "I wish it could be Christmas every day!" The next day, she awoke to the same smells of potatoes and onions frying in the kitchen. She scampered downstairs to see all the gifts surrounding the tree. Her excitement mixed with her family's confusion. Wow! Her wish had come true!

But day after day, Amber's excitement slowly turned into shame. For her little wish had not only affected her family, but all the families in town. She'd only wanted to wake up every day to smell the potatoes, to scamper downstairs in her pajamas and relive the excitement of opening her gifts. But Amber had a secret. She was the one was responsible for this. She made the wish. She was to blame. The townspeople were angry, demanding to know who had caused this to happen. They just wanted to move on with their lives, to wake up and let it be December 26, not Christmas Day all over again.

Turn the page now, and you'd see a big, two-page spread with a huge banner drawn across the notebook, running from one edge to the other. It hung in the middle of the town, and all the townspeople, the animals, even Amber's own family, stood underneath it. The banner read, in big bold red letters, "IT'S AMBER'S FAULT!"

Then ... nothing. That was it. The next and last page simply read, "the end."

I can't help but chuckle to myself now, 30 years later, when I think of my little book. I was so proud of this book. And to be honest, I think the ending was disappointing, to say the least. I don't quite remember why I ended it so abruptly. Maybe I thought I was writing a suspense novel and needed to leave my audience hanging on till the second book was released!

Now, I was just a kid. A creative kid, no doubt. But still, just a kid. Remembering back to that period in my life, I was pretty 'normal.' No major worries. My parents were still married. My sister and I 'bickered,' as my dad used to say, at each other all day. Pretty ordinary family. Pretty ordinary life.

So why the obvious deep-seated image that I was to be held responsible for other people's happiness? Why did I feel shame? Why the insecurity? Why was it 'Amber's Fault'?

For whatever reason—I'm sure I don't know—guilt became my stronghold, even as a young child. And as I grew, it became natural for me to take responsibility for everyone else's feelings, for everyone else's actions, for everyone else's misfortunes or failures. I never took ownership of their happiness, of their successes. No, just bring on the guilt. The line was cast, and the hook of guilt latched on and it's been reeling me in ever since.

Before we can begin to transform our mindset, or more accurately, allow our mindset to *be* transformed, I need you to recognize that, number one, your feelings—no matter what they are—are valid. And number two, that you will need to be honest about them. If not to anyone else, be honest with God, and at the very least, with yourself.

Remember

THERE IS HOPE IN YOUR BROKENNESS

YOU HAVE A CHOICE;
YOU ALWAYS HAVE A CHOICE

Choose to **FEEL** *your emotions,*
ALLOW *your emotions, then* **RELEASE** *them.*

Part III

MINDSET

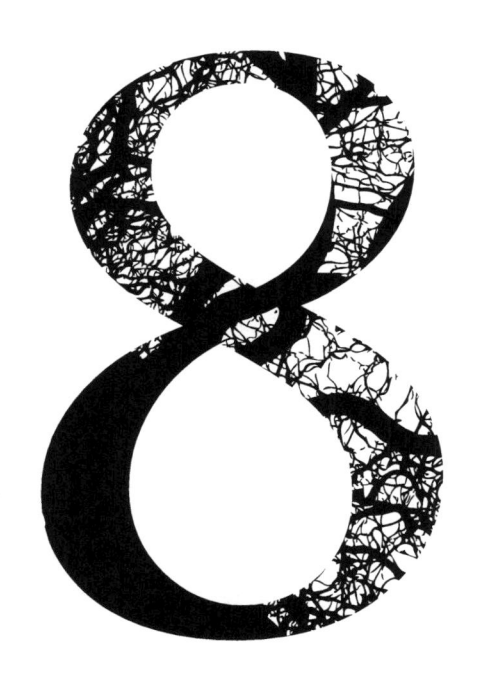

ONE COMMON DENOMINATOR

Owning Your Piece of the Pain

I can distinctively remember feeling such an enormous amount of anxiety over my situation at the time while taking a walk through my neighborhood one afternoon. I'd often grab my earbuds and head outside, either to go for a run or just walk. This was one of those days I knew running wasn't the answer. I navigated to the North Point Community Church app on my phone, earbuds in, and prepared myself to be filled. What I received that day was more than I had bargained for.

Andy Stanley was conducting a series entitled, "Starting Over." I've always enjoyed Stanley's messages simply because, regardless of whether or not you consider yourself to be a Christian, he has this way of pulling out so much practical wisdom from the Bible that it seems almost foolish not to listen. Perfect series for me, since I was just in a 'starting over' phase of my life. Divorce papers filed, and the storms were coming fierce now. Oh, they would get worse for sure, somehow I knew it. Anyway, I found myself immersed in this series, and quite frankly, as I listened on, I was liking less and less what I was hearing.

As I've shared a few pieces of my story with you, you may have found yourself thinking, 'Not exactly the white-picket-fence girl.' You may have even thought, 'Wow, that poor girl.' Might even be safe to assume that my story may have enlisted some pity. If so, let me say, thank you for your compassion. And before taking that walk, filling my head with practical steps to 'start over,' I may have even said 'thank you' and felt comforted by the pity.

But as Stanley rather bluntly pointed out, there is 'one common denominator' in all of your story, in all of your pain, in all of your heartache, in all of your bad situations, breakups, or losses—that one common denominator is: YOU.

It took me a few minutes of listening for the words to really sink in. In my head, I kept saying, "Yeah, but … Yeah, but …"

Have you ever noticed how easy it is to justify what you do or what you have done based on what you want to feel? We don't want to feel any responsibility for our circumstances because, quite frankly, it just doesn't feel good. Furthermore, for months now, I had been hearing repeatedly, "This is all your fault." Just like that book I wrote after Thanksgiving dinner—it's *Amber's Fault*. It was all coming full circle now. Maybe it really *was* all my fault.

Wouldn't it be easier to revert back to the 'yeah, buts' that make us feel a whole lot better? The 'yeah, buts' that justify why we acted in such a way, why we made a poor decision, why we are in the situation we are right now?

> "Owning our story and loving ourselves through the process is the bravest thing that we will ever do." —Brene Brown

I recently came across the following quote by author Brene Brown, which says, "Owning our story and loving ourselves through the process is the bravest thing that we will ever do."

Unfortunate as it may sometimes seem, when we go searching for growth, rest assured we will find ourselves in a situation where we are being forced to grow. I've yet to hear someone tell a story of how they have prayed for growth in an area of their life and God just waved His magic wand, and poof! There you have it—growth! No, instead, we pray for growth, and some of us, like myself that day, even go searching for it. And as a result, what happens is we oftentimes very quickly find ourselves in a set of circumstances where we are being forced to choose: change or remain the same. Or maybe more accurately:

Do or Die

As I was listening to this message, not only was I hearing Andy's words of wisdom being woven into my brain, but I also heard another voice.

Just a few months ago, I had felt a sudden urge to write. It's as if something that should have been obvious all along had just occurred to me. *I have one heck of a story, and I think I need to put this all down on paper.* I didn't really know why at the time, but as it turned out, it proved to become a huge step, though painful, in my healing process, and marked the beginning of my growth. That part of the story was easy. The part where I tell of my parents' divorce, my mother's poor parenting, and all that happened as a result. I've never had a problem talking about that.

But this was different.

By now in my walk, I'd reached a nearby park. I plopped down on a bench, feeling rather overwhelmed with the feelings building up in my heart more and more as I continued to listen. Andy was saying, "Your best bet to a successful future is to own your piece of the past." Well, wait a minute. It wasn't *my* fault my parents got divorced. It wasn't *my* fault my mom brought those guys home. It wasn't *my* fault … it wasn't *my* fault.

You may have a similar past story. You may be able to relate on many levels to my story. Yours might be completely different, but may have resulted in many of the same feelings I've been describing to you. But there is one thing that remains the same throughout each of our stories. We are a part of every single piece of it.

While many of my 'yeah, buts' were fair:

Yes, it's true it wasn't my fault my parents got divorced. Yes, it's true it wasn't my fault my mother brought less than suitable men into our home. Yes, yes, and yes.

The voice I was beginning to hear as I sat on the bench, now sick to my stomach, was, "What part *is* my fault?" When did it stop becoming someone else's fault and start becoming my own?

Could I blame my teenage pregnancy—not one, but two—on my mom? Sure. And some might not blame me for it. Can I blame my own questionable choices in men on my mom's influence? Sure. The list goes on and on. How many of us do this? We give our minds permission to conjure up justifications for the circumstances of our lives, the decisions we've made, the failures we've had. Why? The answer is simple: Because it makes us feel better.

"Your best bet at a successful future is to own your piece of the past." —Andy Stanley

As if owning our piece of our pain isn't bad enough, here comes the hard part. If I were delivering the same message as Andy's, "Your best bet at a successful future is to own your piece of the past," I might have added, "And you don't get to pick and choose which pieces you want to own."

Pick-Up Sticks

Remember the game Pick-Up Sticks? I loved that game as a kid. It's one of those games you can play by yourself. You've got a pile of colored sticks, each about 8 inches long, you drop them down on a flat surface and each player must remove a stick from the pile without disturbing the remaining ones. The winner of the game is the one who has picked up the most sticks. It takes skill and patience and a steady hand to win this game (which is likely why I preferred to play by myself).

I began to realize that this next phase of my growth journey was going to require some serious strategy. If I was going to undertake the task of identifying which sticks to pick up, it meant that I first needed to examine every single other stick in that pile. Anyone who's played the game knows that there's not a single piece that you can pull out of that pile that isn't in some way, either directly or indirectly, dependent on all the other pieces.

Which piece of my story was I willing to own? I decided to take an honest look at my current circumstances. Sure I had been through a lot in my past, growing up. The last few years weren't exactly peachy either. But where was I right now?

Right now, I was going through a divorce. The security I thought I had been providing my kids with by staying in a dysfunctional marriage seemed to be anything but security. Everyone's world seemed to be collapsing. And furthermore, which of the pieces was I willing to take ownership of?

Was I going to stunt my growth or was I going to step forward into it?

Moments of Truth

I made a decision that day. It was 'do or die' time. Was I going to stunt my growth or was I going to step forward into it? I decided to grow. And with this new light having been shed on my ideas of who's to blame, I decided 'do or die' for me meant owning my piece of the pain.

The next day, I contacted my husband. I explained that I'd like to meet him at a park and talk. To say I was scared would be a tremendous understatement. Not to say any divorce is an 'easy' one, but by the end of my almost three-year divorce, I was wishing I had a dollar for everyone who ever claimed to have never witnessed a worse divorce. That being said, I'll simply admit that reaching out to meet with him took more courage than I thought I had. Even as I sat under the pavilion that day, and waited for him, the anxiety I had been feeling for months hit an all-time high.

He showed up and I asked him to agree to two things before the conversation began. I asked that he be kind enough not to interrupt and just allow me to talk. And I asked that he try to listen with an open mind. With a suspicious nod of the head and a roll of the eyes, he agreed. And I began. I spent about an hour that afternoon 'picking up my sticks.' I shared with him every mistake I felt I had made during our marriage, and sincerely apologized for each of those areas. Not once did I mention any of his pieces. I made it clear what my intent was. And in no way was it to cast blame or justify any of the pieces I was willing to own.

I owned my piece of the pain that day. But even more so, I owned pieces of his pain. There were no justifications attached to the pieces. There were no 'yeah, buts.' Just ownership.

I'd love to conclude this chapter with 'and we lived happily ever after.' But choosing to be vulnerable proved to open many more doors to much deeper pain than I had imagined possible. He walked away that day, after proudly proclaiming, "So you finally admit, this is all your fault."

Point missed.

I remember discussing this with my dad prior to my little ownership meeting. He kept shaking his head, warning me that this wasn't a good idea. *This is not going to end how you hope. And anyway, what do you hope to gain from this?*

I was well aware of the likelihood of the meeting ending on a positive note as next to impossible. But yes, I suppose I had hoped that he would indeed listen with an open mind, that he would hear my sincerity and he would forgive me. Those things did not happen that day, but something else much more powerful did.

The most powerful part of owning our piece of the pain, through talking about those pieces that make us feel ashamed or embarrassed, is that it frees us. While it's true that you may find yourself more vulnerable and susceptible to ridicule, you will discover how there is now Grace where there was once Shame.

While your accusers may view you as weak, you can actually boast of your weaknesses. While your accusers may shame you for your weaknesses, you can find grace in a strength much greater than your own, much greater even than your enemies.

> *"But he said to me, 'My grace is sufficient for you, for my power is made perfect in weakness.' Therefore, I will boast all the more gladly about my weaknesses, so that Christ's power may rest on me."*
> —2 Corinthians 12:9

Breaking the Cycle of Pain

What about the pain of my past? What about the pain of *your* past? Have you been carrying pain your whole life, from long, long ago? Maybe you suffered abuse as a child. Maybe you were unwanted. Maybe your dad left you. Maybe your mom never gave you the affirmation you needed. Maybe your teachers or coaches set impossible standards you could never live up to. Maybe you had a brother or sister that seemed to always cast a shadow on you. Maybe you were bullied.

There are certainly situations when you truly are a victim of your circumstances. When I found myself locked in a shed for several days, I was a victim. When my mother constantly ridiculed me and instilled every sense of doubt and worthlessness in me, I was a victim. No, I didn't want for my parents to get divorced. No, I didn't want any part of the aftermath that it brought. I was perfectly content living out the rest of my childhood blissfully happy in what I viewed as *normal*.

But at what point in my story am I no longer a victim? At what point do I start to see a shift take place where my situations become a direct result of my own choices? Do you know what I'm referring to? Does this strike a chord with you? Start thinking about where that shift takes place in your life.

This may be a gray area for you. It is for me. It's surely easier for me to explain I would not have been hanging out on the streets had my mom kept a closer watch over me. If she had given me more attention, I would not have been looking for attention elsewhere. I would have made better choices in friends. Therefore, I would not have driven a drug dealer around, and certainly not all the way to New York City.

And what about my dad? Where was he when all this was going on? Through my younger years before my parents split, my dad was my hero, my idol. I wanted nothing more in life than to be daddy's girl, to be at his side, following his every move.

I remember typing up a letter for my dad. I must have been around 7 years old. This was back in the 'olden days' when there were typewriters—no computers or smart phones. He had just started a new job and I had overheard him talking about it. He didn't seem very happy with the position. So I came up with a great idea (I know, I've been having these great ideas ever since I was a kid). I typed up an anonymous letter and offered to be his friend. He still has it to this day. It read something like this:

> "Dear John, I know you don't like your job and you feel very sad about it. I want to be your friend. If you ever want somebody to talk to, you can write me back, and stick it under a rock outside under the swing set. I'll come pick it up and write back to you. I'll put it back under the rock. I know you must be wondering who this is. I won't ever tell you. But you should know that it's someone who cares about you very much and wants to be your friend."

I could tell stories upon stories of how I adored my dad. I love that he still has the letter. I love that he still has many of my drawings I'd so proudly given him while working next to him in his workshop. I love so many things about my dad. Yet, when I needed him most in my life, he wasn't there.

My parents were far from perfect. Your parents were far from perfect. They made mistakes. And in many homes, they downright failed you. And while my home environment changed drastically, taking a turn for the worse, I have come to understand that much of 'who I am' is a direct reflection of my environment. But that doesn't mean you become any less responsible for who you are today.

The fact is that I chose to mess around with drugs, let alone drive a dealer around in exchange for those drugs. The fact remains that I got pregnant. Not once, but twice. The fact is that I chose to marry a man way before I was anywhere near ready for marriage. Those decisions weren't any more my parents' fault than they were mine.

This game of Pick-Up Sticks may take you much further into your past than you had anticipated. But as Andy Stanley said, "Your best bet at a successful future is to own your piece of the past."

Less Than Perfect

This very important step of owning your piece of the pain is just exactly that: it's painful. It's humbling, to say the least, and may just downright bring you to your knees. But as we will discover in the next chapter, as we continue to grow together, you are, indeed, less than perfect. And furthermore, that's okay. You have been hauling around that heavy wheelbarrow of guilt and shame, for some of you probably your entire life. It's about time you accept that you are less than perfect. I am less than perfect. Your parents were less than perfect. Your ex-husband, ex-wife, your kids, your boss, your teachers, coaches, friends were and still are all less than perfect.

But what you have done for yourself, by owning your piece of the pain and proclaiming that yes, you are less than perfect, is provide healing from past hurts. And here is where our mindsets begin to shift. We can begin to see ourselves, to see our situations, other people's even, through a new filter. Embrace this time to be vulnerable now, own it, and let's get on with the growing.

AMBER NOELLE

Remember

THERE IS HOPE IN YOUR BROKENNESS

YOU HAVE A CHOICE;
YOU ALWAYS HAVE A CHOICE

❦

Choose to **OWN** *your piece of the* **PAIN** *in your story.
After all, it is* **YOUR** *story.*

9

IN THIS CORNER

Guilt vs. Guilty

Do you ever feel guilty? Sure you do. It's safe to say with certainty that you *are* guilty. Before you get offended and put this book down, I'll amend my statement. I am guilty. How's that? Better? But in the spirit of being honest, as I've been challenging you to do throughout this book, let's just assume that you are guilty too.

Guilty of what? You name it. Maybe you cheated on your taxes. Maybe you cheated on your wife or husband. Maybe you lied to your son or maybe you've been keeping a secret so long it's tearing you up inside.

Or maybe it's something much less severe. Maybe you flew through the self-checkout at the grocery store only to get to the car to see that roll of paper towels you forgot to scan in the bottom of the cart. And maybe you were already late to pick up your daughter so you just threw them in your car and left. You told yourself, *I didn't really have time to run back in, and if I just leave them in the cart, someone else would take them anyway.* No matter where our guilt stems from, no matter how big or small the offense, we all feel it at times.

And it feels terrible. Especially those more severe offenses—it's likely we all have at least one. It keeps nagging at us. Constant. Unrelenting. Over and over again, replaying in our minds. Creating regret and shame. And of course, accompanied by anxiety. Your mind starts racing with all the 'what ifs.' What if he finds out? What if they all find out? What if that growing crowd of accusers all know what happened, what you did, what you said? Anxiety, fear, denial, justification—they all start to create a sort of funnel in our mind, spiraling downward until we find ourselves becoming someone we never wanted to become.

So what exactly is guilt? Guilt is an awareness of having done something wrong. It's simple. But you already know what guilt is. All of us have either done wrong things or we have failed to do right things; therefore, all of us have experienced guilt. What makes situations differ is *how* we respond to guilt.

Guilty Confessions

In the spirit of being honest, I'm about to become about as vulnerable as I've been with you thus far. I'd like to share with you a piece of my story that I oftentimes pass over. It gets an honorable mention, but never ends up being showcased. I'd like to introduce you to Guilt, in this corner of my own life.

Back in Chapter 4, I told a story of one of the many defining moments in my life that began to shape who I perceived myself to be. I was a failure—not once, but twice. I was pregnant again. I told the story from the perspective of discovery, that moment I realized all the uncertainties that lay ahead of me. And that's how I ended *that* story. But of course, there's more. There's always more.

My already poor sense of self-worth, my already diminished hope of being of any value to anyone, was becoming hardened, 'set in stone' as some might say. There was no convincing me otherwise. I was guilty. I had made another poor choice. And I was quickly about to make even more.

Days went by after finding out the news. I was in a complete sense of panic. Here I was, barely past 18. Living on my own. About to graduate with an associate's degree. Trying to find a job so I can get off government support and provide for the son I already had.

Before that day, I remember feeling a tiny sense of pride. It wasn't much, but for the first time in a very long time, I remember looking at my son, just a year and a half old, and thinking, "Wow. I'm really doing it. I'm really making something of myself. I'm really being a good mom." It felt pretty good, I must say.

Maybe that's why this news hit me so hard. It was as if my balloon was slowly starting to inflate, just barely getting off the ground when bam!—a bird swooped in and popped my balloon. I'm not talking about just some bird. Picture *Tucan Sam*. (If you know who I'm talking about, you too are a child of the '80s.) *Oh yeah, that's right—I'm nothing but a screw-up, a repeat failure.*

What was my reaction? Initially, it was panic. Then quickly followed by, *What do I do now? What will everyone think? How am I going to get through this?* My mind started racing—not forward, but backward. I began to replay every screw-up I'd ever had.

> I thought about how my sweet baby boy used to cling to me when I dropped him off at day care. I thought about how I used to go visit him during my lunch break from school, and again, he'd cling to me. And for having to leave him there, I felt guilt.

> I thought about his father and how if I had just been a better girlfriend, maybe we'd still be together. I felt guilt.

> I thought about my dad and the ladies at his church, who would drive out every night to take turns staying with my son while I went to work in the evening after a day at school. I felt guilt.

> I thought about my mom spending countless nights crying in her room when she was alone again. I felt guilt.

I thought about my sister, and how I was mean to her because I resented her for having something with my mom that I didn't. I felt guilt.

I thought about the look in my dad's eyes and the heaviness in his heart when I told him I was pregnant the first time, after he just suffered the loss of his parents. I felt guilt.

I thought about how I stole attention from my mom's boyfriend, and how it ultimately caused her pain because he left. I felt guilt.

I thought way back to my parents' divorce. I wondered what I could have done to help but didn't. I felt guilt.

This had become somewhat of a daily routine for me. Throughout the day, whether at school or at work, or while lying in my bed at night, my mind would wander all around as if searching for more reasons to feel guilty. It was almost as if I needed guilt to feel normal.

But that day, peering down at another positive pregnancy test, this guilt took me to a whole new level. That level was panic. Pure panic.

So I lied.

And here began the first of many steps away from growth, the first of many steps away from healing. I began thinking to myself, *how can I make this better for myself, or how can I become a victim rather than the offender?* At this point in my life, I didn't give much conscious thought to any impulses I had. I didn't know how to. Everything was derived from an impulsive reaction. And that impulsive response resulted in a lie.

I told people I was raped. Yes. I lied. Not just a small white lie. But a terrible lie. Of course, all of the accompanying details were made up as well. I didn't take time to really think this through, to plan for any follow-up questions that might arise from such a shocking revelation. No, I just 'winged it.' Then came the big question—the one question I surely didn't prepare myself to answer. "What are you going to do? You aren't going to keep the baby are you?"

Suddenly, a new panic set in. New guilt. Abortion? I had never, would never, consider it. But suddenly, I found myself considering it. It was an easy way out. It was surely justified, considering I had been raped. But wait, that's right—I *hadn't* been raped. What do I do now? No one would fault me. And let's get real here, it was hard enough being just a kid myself trying to raise one baby. How could I possibly handle *two* babies?

After only a few weeks had passed, I awoke to my dad calling me. He asked me to come to church. I hadn't been to church in what seemed like forever. After all, where had God been anyway? I sure hadn't seen Him lately. He wasn't rushing to my aid, answering any of my requests. But whatever. I thought, *sure, why not.* So I got up and grabbed my Bible, which happened to be in a box, collecting dust under my bed. And along with it, I grabbed a 'Bible promises' book my dad had given me years ago.

As I sat in church that day, not even listening to the message, I found myself staring at my son sleeping so peacefully on my lap. I thought about the baby he once was, forming in my belly. And then I thought of the new life forming in my belly right that minute, unbeknownst to anyone whom I hadn't told. I reached over and picked up the promise book. Flipping through the pages, I came across this verse:

> *"No temptation has overtaken you except what is common to mankind. And God is faithful; he will not let you be tempted beyond what you can bear. But when you are tempted, he will also provide a way out so that you can endure it."*
> —1 Corinthians 10:13

In that very moment, I knew I would not only have this baby but that I would surely be okay. Not just be okay, but I would be a good mom. Not just a good mom, but a better mom than mine. I would be strong. I would be brave. I would be bigger than I thought I was, better than I thought I was. Yes, I would have this baby. And somehow, this God, who didn't seem to care who I was, or even know my name, was going to provide a way for me to endure anything that lay ahead in my path.

I cried. Once again, I held my son close to my heart, his little beating heart next to mine, sleeping so peacefully, so securely in my arms. I was his everything. And I suddenly felt that same kind of love doubled, as if I were now holding both of my babies in my arms. I loved this baby—my baby, my son. And I loved this new life growing inside me—my baby, my son.

I confessed my lie to my family. Oddly enough, they seemed to know I hadn't been honest about the pregnancy. Funny how a poorly planned story ultimately always has holes. And funny how everyone can see them but you.

In the month of July that following year, I gave birth to a baby boy, just a week shy of my dad's birthday. Not just any baby boy, but the boy I like to think of as my 'surrender baby.' I surrendered the idea of my own ability that day several months ago on the church pew, and I gave God full permission to follow through on His promise to me, to provide a way of endurance.

He was absolutely beautiful. I named him after my dad. I gave him my dad's last name. He would be a 'third.' What my dad didn't know that day in the hospital as he looked down at his grandson, now bearing his name, was that in one way, one very important way, he was holding that baby that day because he had invited me to church. And he had given me that little Bible promises book years prior.

It wasn't until months later and the years to come that I would begin to feel the kind of guilt that would eat away at me in a way that I would have never dreamed.

Less than a year after my second son was born, I met a man who would later become my husband. As I shared earlier, he instantly connected with my older son. And while my older son had not had any contact with his father at the time, he remembered him. He knew this new man in his mom's life was not his dad. My baby, on the other hand, grew through the years believing this man was his father. He had never known any differently. My older son had started referring to my husband as 'dad,' and naturally, his little brother followed suit.

As the years passed and preschool was quickly approaching, my husband and I decided together that we would simply make a 'correction' on his birth certificate. We would list a father. We would list my husband.

But something felt so wrong. I knew this wasn't right—another lie, another deception. But it was easy enough to justify, to convince myself this was the best thing to do, and even going so far as to convince myself that this was best for my son. In reality, even that was a justification. Truth be told, I thought that this would not only make things 'easier' for my son, but it would also make things easier for me. I could hide my guilt even further by not having to answer questions regarding his last name.

More time passed. I grew more and more anxious. This was the one single thing that plagued my thoughts day in and day out. There was not a day that I did not think about the deception that I had created. There was not a day that I didn't long to tell my son the truth. *But why?* I reminded myself that it was better for him not to know. Over time, with every single passing wedding anniversary, the guilt and anxiety continued to grow. Wouldn't my son start doing the math, start putting together a timeline and wonder at what point exactly he came into the picture? Something wouldn't match up, between his date of birth and our anniversary date. But still, I never spoke of it and he never asked. I continued to harbor this secret while year after year, it ate away at me. I wanted so badly to tell him.

Then came the day I told my son my secret. By this time, he was 12 years old. My divorce was well underway. As a result, all three of my children were suffering in ways I had never imagined that day I said 'I do' 11 years ago. There was a lot of resentment and anger in my now-crumbling marriage, and my sons were getting the brunt of the dysfunction. A phone call from my oldest son one day brought me to the decision to share my secret with them both. He had questions. He had been hearing things that just weren't computing in his brain, such as the not-so-subtle hints that not only was he not my husband's son, which he was well aware of, but that his younger brother was not his stepfather's son either.

The month prior to my son's inquiry, I had been receiving threats that my husband would tell my son the 'truth.' The truth, as he saw it, was that I was a whore, that my son was a mistake, that I am a liar. My husband's version of the story was certainly not one that I wanted for either of my boys or my daughter to hear.

I picked up both of my boys, brought them home, and after praying with my dad, I decided to sit my two boys down, now 12 and 14, and tell them my deep dark secret, tell them the truth. So with my dad by my side, and my boys settled on the living room couch, I pulled up an ottoman across from them, and proceeded to tell them a story that I knew would bring even more devastation to their fragile and crumbling world. But nonetheless, a story that I knew they needed to hear directly from me. It was, after all, my story to tell.

"Boys," I said, "I need to talk to you. I need to tell you something very important."

I had, at different times and for different reasons, shared bits of my past with them. I proceeded to tell them much of what they already knew. As I came to the part where I told of my oldest son's birth and I described how much I loved him, I started to get emotional. This is where the story was going to get complicated. How do I tell them something that will break their hearts, but that ultimately needed to be told?

By now, I was having difficulty talking, and my dad was tearing up. My sweet boys looked at me, and then my youngest son said, "It's okay Mom, you don't have to talk about it. We already know all this." I leaned in close, and said, "But there's more."

"The part of the story that you don't know is that about a year later, I got pregnant again." I paused for a moment, letting this sink in, giving them time to process it. My oldest son looked at me now as if he knew exactly where I was going with this, as if the not-so-subtle hints he had been hearing for the last few weeks were suddenly making sense now. And my dear sweet 12-year-old son asked, "You mean I have another brother or sister out there?"

"Oh sweetheart," I said, leaning in closer, "I was pregnant with you."

I went on to explain in great detail the deep love I felt for my oldest son, how I had not imagined I could feel any more love in my heart than that. And then, he was born. I told how my love overflowed then at that moment for both of my sons. I explained every last little detail of the day he was born, from his perfectly round head to his perfect eyebrows, the way he looked at me, the way I held him, the indescribable feeling of gratefulness I felt in my heart that I had been blessed with this beautiful baby boy. How he was far beyond what I deserved, but that I was so blessed to have him, to have both of them, and how honored I was to be their mother.

I was crying. My younger son got up, sat next to me, and put his arms around me. We cried in each other's embrace. He kept telling me he loved me.

With such shame, I explained that I didn't know much about his father. I admitted that I didn't even remember his name. I tried to explain how bad a place I was in, that I had made poor decision after poor decision, but that he was not a mistake. He was a gift. One of the three greatest gifts I had ever been given. I glanced over at my oldest son. He was always the 'serious' one, always being strong for everyone. I looked him in the eye, asked him if he's okay and if he had any questions. He leaned forward, grabbed my hand, and simply said, "Mom. I love you. You're still the same mom. You're still the same person to me." What beautiful hearts these two young boys have. Truly, what amazing hearts.

I continue on, explaining that they may have many questions. They may not understand everything. At times they may hate me, at times they may resent me. But I assured them, it was okay. It was okay if they got mad at me, it was okay if they told me about it. I would love them unconditionally, no matter what they felt toward me. I also explained how much my husband loved them from the very beginning. I asked them to be patient, to try to be understanding of their stepfather's behavior. He had been hurting, too—I had hurt him by leaving the marriage. He was angry and dealing with a whirlwind of emotions, too. I explained that I was so sorry to have kept this a secret for so long, how badly I had wanted to tell them. And despite the fact that I was not 'allowed' to tell them, it was no excuse. I had never had the courage to do so, never was able to do what I knew had to be done. I apologized that the time had to be now, in the midst of all they were already experiencing. But I wanted—*needed*—them to know that they were loved, that they had to hear the story from their mother and no one else.

False Guilt

Why did I choose to share this piece of my story with you?

While there is no harm in speaking about the pieces of ourselves that we are proud of, this does little more than inflate our own egos, or even worse, allow us to continue hiding from our guilt, from our shame. My intent in sharing this story with you is two-fold.

The first is simply this, broken down into three, very distinct categories:

You can *feel* guilty and *not be* guilty.
You can *feel* guilty and *be* guilty.
You can *be* guilty and *not feel* guilty.

Which category would you like to be in? Well, of course, the one that's not listed. The one where we are *not guilty*, and therefore, *do not feel* guilty. But hopefully we have already moved past the stage of denial and we are now taking a hard look at the areas of our lives where we *are indeed guilty* or where we are *feeling* guilty, but we aren't sure whether or not we truly are.

We've identified what guilt is. It is an awareness of having done something wrong. But herein lies the real question surrounding the word 'guilt.' Who gets to decide what's wrong or not wrong? Guilt comes from not living up to someone's standards. So whose standards are we going by?

One of the most amazing pieces of the story of The Toy Maker is easily glossed over. Remember that as the story came to an end, as the children were preparing to leave the orphanage, they came downstairs one last time as they heard the reminiscent chime of the doorbell? Remember as their heads hung low, their faces covered with guilt and shame? Behind their backs, they were holding their battered and seemingly worthless toy. They had truly been guilty of mistreating their toy over the years.

But here comes the amazing part, the part so easily overlooked. It's found in the Toy Maker's response. As the children shamefully presented their damaged toy to its maker, the Toy Maker didn't scowl at the children nor scold them. No. With those big brown kind eyes, and with anticipation, he asked, "But have you discovered the special feature?"

I can imagine the children's initial reaction. At the very least, they were probably thinking it: "Why isn't he mad? Why doesn't he seem to care that we haven't taken such good care of his gift?" It's so beautiful; it's as if all the Toy Maker was concerned about was whether or not the children received what he had specially intended for them all along. He then embraced the children. And even more than that, he explained that he had a solution for their seemingly broken toy. He would fix it up, good as new. No guilt. No shame. No payment needed for their wrongdoing.

Is my story any different from this? Is yours? I will never forget the blessing I received that day while sitting in my living room, sharing my deepest secret with my two boys. Even as young children, they didn't shame me. They didn't see in me what I had been seeing for so long. Their perception of me was much different from my own. No. They leaned in close, grabbed my hand, and simply said, "Mom, I love you. Nothing will ever change that."

Is it possible that while you've been dragging around this tractor-trailer load of guilt and shame, it wasn't your load to carry all along? That it was false guilt? There may have been pieces of that load that were yours to carry, but the whole load? Likely not.

I found freedom that day. Not only in releasing the secret that burned inside me, but I found freedom in the response of my two boys. They didn't see the tractor-trailer load behind me. They only saw me, the 'same mom,' as they put it, that they had always seen.

Freedom in the Cure

Have you identified some areas of your life—maybe one, two, or even many decisions you've made—that brought about guilt, and rightfully so? Not a great feeling, I know. It feels downright horrible. Shame is a painful feeling. Guilty actions result in a loss of respect by others, a direct consequence of our own choices. And that results in the painful feeling of shame we've all experienced to some degree.

Guilt is related to what we do while shame is much deeper than that. Shame defines *who we are*, going beyond just what we do.

What if there was a way to not *feel* guilty, to not *feel* shame even if there is a valid reason to?

What if the answer was a whole lot less complicated than you thought? It is. It boils down to this: You make a choice.

Simple solution, though not as easy as it sounds.

I reflect back to my first 'book' where throughout the story, I innocently asked for something. I just wanted it to be Christmas every day. What's the big deal, really? Wouldn't everyone want that? But as the story unfolded, the entire town, my family, even the bunnies and squirrels, blamed me. It's a cute story, sure, even comical. But what an amazing discovery this brought about. I had always felt guilty. It was, in a way, as some might say, part of my 'wiring.'

Maybe you're one of those people who have the ability to simply acknowledge their guilt. You even go so far as to ask forgiveness from anyone you may have wronged. And then, as if it never happened, you just 'let it go.' There's no anxiety associated with your guilty actions. There's no shame casting a shadow on your every move. If so, maybe this hasn't been a stronghold in your life.

I'd venture to say that for many of us, unfortunately, that's not the case. We have all been born with an innate desire to feel accepted, to feel loved, to feel needed, to feel appreciated. But what happens when we don't feel loved or accepted? When we don't feel good enough or worthy? That's when our 'wiring' comes into play. And if you're anything like me, if you can relate to this feeling of guilt and shame following you around your entire life, simply choosing to 'let it go' is not so simple.

You keep beating yourself up. You allow other people to beat you up. If you are like me, this is true regardless of what category you fall into—whether you are guilty or not. You take on guilt and shame as if you know no other way.

Choice. You're thinking, 'Choice, you say.' You're skeptical, and you have reason to be. You've tried to let it go. You've tried hiding. You've tried justifying. You've tried denying. What is there left to do but just live out the rest of your miserable existence feeling this way? I hear you. I've been there. And yes, because I've fought against this my whole life, I am *still* there, right here with you.

Accept, Believe, Surrender

First, accept your guilt. Acknowledge that you cannot hide it, cover it up, or ignore it. But God sees it.

In Hebrews 4:12-13, we read, *"For the word of God is alive and active. Sharper than any double-edged sword, it penetrates even to dividing soul and spirit, joints and marrow; it judges the thoughts and attitudes of the heart. Nothing in all creation is hidden from God's sight. Everything is uncovered and laid bare before the eyes of him to whom we must give account."*

Not very comforting, is it? In the short term, it may seem easier to hide, ignore, cover up. But if we truly want freedom from our guilt and shame for the long term, we cannot avoid this acknowledgment that God has seen it. You are held accountable. It no longer matters what you tell yourself. It no longer matters what someone else tells you. God sees it.

Next, you have to enter into belief. This is the part where faith comes into play. And faith, by definition, is a choice. According to the dictionary, faith is a belief that is not based on proof.

But as it relates to God, consider this as being a more accurate definition:

> Faith is a conscious choice we make to believe, which oftentimes develops into proof based on our own personal experience with the very thing or person we chose to have faith in.

Again, I remind you, I am no scholar, which is why I simply ask you to consider my humble attempt at defining faith as a possible alternative view of the concept. This is how I've experienced the power of faith in my own life.

The author of Hebrews continues in verses 14-16: *"Therefore, since we have a great high priest who has ascended into heaven, Jesus the Son of God, let us hold firmly to the faith we profess. For we do not have a high priest who is unable to empathize with our weaknesses, but we have one who has been tempted in every way, just as we are—yet he did not sin. Let us then approach God's throne of grace with confidence, so that we may receive mercy and find grace to help us in our time of need."*

While there are many Scriptures relating to the subject of guilt and shame, I personally believe that we have to first accept Jesus for who He is. And furthermore, for the authority He holds because of His own blameless life. But here's the real mind-blowing revelation: while it is true that He was never guilty of any sin, He has felt the same temptations and has suffered from the same human weaknesses. But He overcame. How, you ask? Simple. By choice.

So, that's great, you're thinking. *Jesus can resist. But how can I?* One word: Surrender.

In John 3:17-18, we read, *"For God did not send His Son into the world to condemn the world, but that the world through Him might be saved. He who believes in Him is not condemned; but he who does not believe is condemned already, because he has not believed in the name of the only begotten Son of God."*

Earlier in this book, when we talked about our feelings being valid, I asked you, "Who are you listening to?" I didn't really go into much detail beyond just posing the question. So I'm asking you again, "Who are you listening to?"

If you aren't really too sure about God, if you feel like He hasn't come through for you yet, why start trusting Him now? To that question, this is my response: "What have you got to lose?" At this point, you've likely been carrying this guilt, wearing this shame, for much longer than you've ever imagined. You're already over halfway through this book; why not give it a shot?

I've been honest with you. I've been vulnerable with you, as I promised. I realize the risk involved just in writing this book. I realize the criticism that will surely follow. As I continue to share and to open my life up to hundreds, maybe thousands, who now have a front row seat to my less-than-perfect life, I am well aware of the consequences that will likely follow. And let me assure you, I'm not looking forward to them. But, all that being said, I am still willing to bring myself to this level of vulnerability. Why? Because what I found to be true about *faith*—not only as the dictionary describes it, but through evidence in my own life—is that God is real. And there is deliverance and hope in our surrendering to Him. And all that is likely to follow as a result of this book is worth it even if only one person can find hope through everything I've shared.

This surrender is what will enable us to suddenly see the guilt and shame we carry as a choice.

This surrender is what will enable us to suddenly see the guilt and shame we carry as a choice. We can somehow magically turn it off, let it go. No longer hide it, no longer ignore it, no longer deny it. But truly and wholeheartedly, *let it go*.

You can conjure up all kinds of creative ways to try to rid yourself of these feelings. But you already know your guilt goes far beyond just a feeling. It really has to do with your relationship with God. Choosing to release guilt will ultimately depend on how you view God and how you choose to relate with Him in your life.

Not a quick and painless process, I assure you. I am still very much in the growing phase of this process myself. I never promised you easy. I never promised you quick. But I did promise you authenticity, and I did promise you a solution. Maybe not the solution for you, but a solution nonetheless. So why not try it? It might just work for you. It has worked for me and continues to work for me as I steadily march forward in this journey of growth.

Remember

THERE IS HOPE IN YOUR BROKENNESS

YOU HAVE A **CHOICE**;
YOU **ALWAYS** HAVE A CHOICE

⁕

Choose to **SURRENDER** *your guilt and shame.*
Choose to **ACCEPT** *forgiveness from the*
only true source of **REDEMPTION.**

10

FALSE 'FACTS'

Can You Handle the Truth?

Let's begin this chapter by acknowledging that your results thus far are no reflection of what your true potential is. We've already discovered that we subconsciously develop a perception of who we are. And it's safe to say we've also discovered that much, if not all, of that perception is based on the beliefs and opinions of other people. John Moore says, *"Your opinion is your opinion. Your perception is your perception. Do not confuse them with facts or truth."*

One of my favorite quotes comes from Mark Twain. He says, *"Education consists mainly of what we have unlearned."*

"Your opinion is your opinion. Your perception is your perception. Do not confuse them with facts or truth." –John Moore

---

What are some 'facts' that have been ingrained in us throughout the last several months, years—for many of us, our whole lives? What have we simply accepted as fact, no questions asked? That it 'is what it is'?

If we want to truly see our mindset transform, we are going to have to unveil some of these false 'facts.' You must commit to open your mind up and allow something—or more accurately, *someone*—to rewire your conscious mind.

5 False 'Facts' Overruled

#1
I am Guilty and Unworthy
CORRECTION: I AM FORGIVEN

But you, Lord, are a compassionate and gracious God, slow to anger, abounding in love and faithfulness.
—Psalm 86:15

Do not judge, and you will not be judged. Do not condemn, and you will not be condemned. Forgive, and you will be forgiven.
—Luke 6:37

Therefore, there is now no condemnation for those who are in Christ Jesus, because through Christ Jesus the law of the Spirit who gives life has set you free from the law of sin and death.
—Romans 8:1-2

If we confess our sins, he is faithful and just and will forgive us our sins and purify us from all unrighteousness.
—1 John 1:9

#2
I am Weak and a Coward
CORRECTION: I AM STRONG AND COURAGEOUS

Be strong and courageous. Do not be afraid or terrified because of them, for the Lord your God goes with you; he will never leave you nor forsake you … The Lord himself goes before you

and will be with you; he will never leave you nor forsake you. Do not be afraid; do not be discouraged.
—Deuteronomy 31:6, 8

I sought the Lord, and he answered me; he delivered me from all my fears.
—Psalm 34:4

Keep your lives free from the love of money and be content with what you have, because God has said, "Never will I leave you; never will I forsake you."
—Hebrews 13:5

Now go; I will help you speak and will teach you what to say.
—Exodus 4:12

#3
I am Scared and Alone
CORRECTION: I AM PROTECTED AND NEVER ALONE

I am with you and will watch over you wherever you go, and I will bring you back to this land. I will not leave you until I have done what I have promised you.
—Genesis 28:15

Even though I walk through the darkest valley, I will fear no evil, for you are with me; your rod and your staff, they comfort me.
—Psalm 23:4

God is our refuge and strength, an ever-present help in trouble. Therefore, we will not fear, though the earth give way and the mountains fall into the heart of the sea.
—Psalm 46:1-2

What, then, shall we say in response to these things? If God is for us, who can be against us?
—Romans 8:31

He will wipe every tear from their eyes. There will be no more death or mourning or crying or pain, for the old order of things has passed away.
—Revelation 21:4

#4
I am Lost and Confused
CORRECTION: I HAVE DIRECTION AND WISDOM

I will instruct you and teach you in the way you should go; I will counsel you with my loving eye on you.
—Psalm 32:8

Trust in the Lord with all your heart and lean not on your own understanding; in all your ways submit to him, and he will make your paths straight.
—Proverbs 3:5-6

You will seek me and find me when you seek me with all your heart.
—Jeremiah 29:13

Ask and it will be given to you; seek and you will find; knock and the door will be opened to you.
—Matthew 7:7

Finally, brothers and sisters, whatever is true, whatever is noble, whatever is right, whatever is pure, whatever is lovely, whatever is admirable—if anything is excellent or praiseworthy—think about such things.
—Philippians 4:8

If any of you lacks wisdom, you should ask God, who gives generously to all without finding fault, and it will be given to you.
—James 1:5

#5
I am Tired and Worn Out
CORRECTION: I AM RESTORED AND WILL PERSEVERE

I can do all this through him who gives me strength.
—Philippians 4:13

Come to me, all you who are weary and burdened, and I will give you rest.
—Matthew 11:28

Consider it pure joy, my brothers and sisters, whenever you face trials of many kinds, because you know that the testing of your faith produces perseverance. Let perseverance finish its work so that you may be mature and complete, not lacking anything.
—James 1:2-4

No temptation has overtaken you except what is common to mankind. And God is faithful; he will not let you be tempted beyond what you can bear. But when you are tempted, he will also provide a way out so that you can endure it.
—1 Corinthians 10:13

Jesus replied, "What is impossible with man is possible with God."
—Luke 18:27

Remember

THERE IS **HOPE** IN YOUR **BROKENNESS**

YOU HAVE A **CHOICE;**
YOU **ALWAYS** HAVE A CHOICE

❦

Choose **FAITH** *in the certainty of* **UNCERTAINTY.**

Part IV

HOPE & PERSEVERANCE

11

ACCEPT THIS CANCER

The Promise of Blessing

It was July of 2014, over two years into one of the most difficult seasons of my life thus far. My divorce had proven to take much longer than I would have ever anticipated. I had spent the last three years hearing over and over again, in my already 'guilt-wired' head, *this is your fault. This divorce, this failed marriage*. But even worse than that, the words that cut deeper than any others through these years were, not only is this disaster of a divorce my fault, but furthermore, all of the problems my children now face, all of their 'mess-ups' and their struggles, are all my fault as well.

The shame of my past was continually being thrown in my face. There had been threats, although more accurately presented as 'promises' that I would surely suffer these horrible things again, and even worse. I'd hear these words repeated over and over again with a sense of anticipation and pride, as if watching me suffer through physical and sexual abuse again, as if seeing my own children suffer, would somehow bring about some sort of justice for all the pain I had seemingly caused.

I had been pleading with God to rid me of my own pain, begging Him to just make it stop. *Please, for the sake of my kids, for my own sake, please just make it all stop.*

But one summer day in July—I remember it very well—my family was visiting from Tennessee. My sweet little nieces always brought me such joy. It was good to have these young, innocent, and happy little rays of sunshine running around in my house, in my backyard, just kind of brightening everyone's mood. It had been so stressful—so much fear, so much drama, so much anxiety—that it was a breath of fresh air to have them here to visit.

On this particular day, I was even more grateful to have my family with me. As I walked in the door from a doctor's visit, I was happy to have my sister there, to hold me as I cried out my fear in her arms. I had found a lump in my breast. I was sure my doctor would tell me it was nothing to worry about. But instead, he ordered an ultrasound. He tried not to seem concerned, but the look in his eyes said otherwise.

I remember going home, trying to keep it together. I remember looking up at God, thinking, "Really? Seriously? As if I don't have enough going on. I do not need this right now."

A few weeks passed by, and August came. I was impatiently waiting on results from a biopsy. While they had not been concerned about the lump I had discovered, the ultrasound showed another lump which did indeed raise some concern. To put it lightly, let's just say I wasn't feeling on good terms with God at that moment. My children were going through so much, and here I was, doing all I could to keep them afloat. Meanwhile, as if the stress and pressure of the divorce weren't enough, God allowed this threat of cancer in my life. Why? I just didn't understand it.

So when a reminder popped up on my calendar for the Global Leadership Summit I had registered for months ago, I was in no mood to go. But hey, I paid for it, so I decided to go. Notebook in hand, I sat down. I murmured a half-hearted prayer—something along the lines of, "Okay God, I'm here. Talk to me if You want to, or whatever." I was downright angry. I did not deserve this. I was not happy about it. I had been faithful to God. I had been listening to Him. I had been searching for Him, been growing, been praying. Why this? And why *now*?

This is the part of the story where I start to sound a little 'off my rocker.' But in the spirit of being vulnerable, I'll go on. What I experienced that day was unlike anything I had ever encountered. It makes me sound a little crazy, and quite honestly, back then, I was beginning to wonder if I was indeed losing my marbles.

Immediately after I said my pathetic prayer, I felt a sort of chill come over me. I hardly heard anything; the sounds in the auditorium were muffled. I opened my eyes, picked my head up, and all of my senses were dulled. All except one. My subconscious mind seemed to be accessible in a way that I'd never experienced before. Meanwhile, my conscious mind was no longer calling the shots. Something within my subconscious was communicating with me, and very clearly. Yes, I know I'm sounding more and more crazy with each passing paragraph. But bear with me.

I heard very distinctly, as if someone were sitting right next to me, speaking to me. "Amber, start writing. I have something to say to you."

I had oftentimes, in the last few years, discovered that God seems to speak to me through my writing. Many nights I'd awake with an overwhelming need to 'start writing.' But every time, up until this moment, although my thoughts seemed to be inspired, I had never heard so clearly as I did in that moment. And so, without hesitation, I grabbed my notebook and started writing, excitement coursing through me because I fully believed God was about to reveal that I didn't have cancer and all was going to be okay. I thought, *So yes! Bring it on, I'm ready to hear this!*

But instead, I heard, "Amber, you have cancer. And I want you to be happy about it." I stopped, shook my head, and thought, *I must be hearing wrong.* As if this assurance of cancer wasn't bad enough, I'm supposed to be *happy* about it? Not *okay* with it, not *content* with it. No. *Happy.* I was supposed to be happy.

Again, I heard the same thing repeated. Then, "Listen, I have great plans for you. But this cancer is something you must endure for Me to take you where I want you to go."

Still listening. By now, all of my senses had completely tuned out. This voice was all I could hear. "Amber, you've been complaining about your life, you've referred to your journey as 'wandering in the wilderness.' Amber, you've been desperate to get to the 'promised land,' to discover your purpose. Well, this cancer—this is what is going to bring you over to the other side."

Wow. Not at all what I was expecting.

After a brief pause, as if the voice was patiently allowing this all to sink in, "Do you accept? Will you accept this cancer? You must be willing to be happy about it."

"Yes … Yes, I accept. And yes, I will choose to be happy about it."

Somehow I knew simply accepting it was not enough. God was asking me to be happy in the suffering He was purposely placing in my life. For the next few hours, I found myself writing frantically. I had no awareness of anything else going on around me in that auditorium. The next thing I heard was, "Now pick your head up. You see that woman speaking on stage? That is what I have for you. That is your purpose. You are going to tell your story, Amber."

For the remainder of my time there that day, I wrote and wrote. I couldn't tell you what I was writing. Simply put, I had no idea. I was just writing. It wasn't until I left the church, walked out to the parking lot, and sat in my car, trying to gather my emotions, that I first read all I had written that day. And lo and behold, it was a rough, scatter-brained-style outline of what I was to speak about, what pieces of my story to share.

A few weeks after that experience, I was waiting for my test results. By now, I had fully accepted this cancer. I was actually happy about it. I can only imagine how insensitive that sounds to anyone who has battled cancer themselves or watched a loved one go through it, or even worse, have experienced loss due to cancer. It's certainly not something to be happy about. And while I can't say I was happy about the certainty of this disease and all the suffering it would surely bring, I was choosing to be happy about what lay ahead of me. It didn't matter to me anymore what I had to go through. If God was willing to reveal His purpose for me through this cancer, then for that, I was certainly happy. Excited even.

So you can imagine my confusion when I received the phone call. "Good news," I heard on the other line, "all your tests came back negative."

So here I was once again, looking up at God and saying, "Really? Seriously?" I had just spent the last few weeks not only mentally preparing myself for what was ahead, but surrendering my emotions to God and allowing Him to replace any fear or anxiety I had with happiness. Yes, I was happy. Now, I was left confused and frustrated. And yes, of course, feeling guilty. Feeling shame for being disappointed that I *don't* have cancer.

I spent the next day back on my knees, asking God what exactly He was up to. I know what I heard. I felt it more strongly than anything I had ever felt in my life. I wasn't going crazy. I know it. But still, I had no answers.

It is now almost two years later, and while I routinely go through the screening process, I do not have cancer—yet. But I can tell you this one thing I've discovered in this experience: God has a sense of humor. At my last doctor appointment, they told me, "Your tests came out great, Amber." So then I was wondering, "Okay, then why have me drive over an hour to your office just to hear good news?" The nurse took over, explaining to me, "But … we have discovered a broken gene. We can't tell you much about it—not much at all. You see, in over 12 years of testing—around the world—you are the first person with this positive test result … this broken gene."

I can remember staring right past her, as if, once again, all my other senses were going numb, like what she was saying wasn't quite computing in my brain. Then I looked right at her and smiled. She tried to provide me reassurance that through regular testing, they will surely detect any cancer in the very early stages. I'm sure she was confused by my reaction.

I left the office that day, chuckling to myself. God surely does have a sense of humor. It's as if He was saying to me, "Amber, I told you. I just didn't tell you when. Just in case you forgot, I just thought I'd remind you to trust Me." As odd as it may seem, and even insensitive to those who have suffered through cancer, I am not afraid.

Furthermore, I am not only unafraid, I am actually *happy* in the waiting.

Blessing in the Promise of Pain

You see, sometimes you may hear from God, or you may think you hear from God. And you're all-in. You're ready to accept the cancer. You're ready to accept the struggle that lies ahead. But somewhere along the way, you grow weary, tired of waiting for the promised 'blessing.'

What happens when you say 'yes' to cancer? You agree to be happy about some struggle that hasn't even come yet. Meanwhile, there is constant, continual struggle coming at you from every direction—struggle you *didn't* see coming. Struggle God *didn't* tell you about. But still haunting you in the back of your mind is the greater struggle that is yet to come, the greater struggle that has been foretold to you. What then?

What happens when, while you're waiting, you begin to experience even greater heartbreak. What then?

Oftentimes, we will find ourselves trying to drift back into a 'safe zone,' a place that isn't so painful, a place where life is blissful. Problem is, the storms don't stop, and we're left with a decision. What are we going to do with the struggle, with the pain? Are we going to accept the struggle and seek to find what God's purpose is in it? Or are we going to frantically do an about-face and run in the other direction?

While option number two may seem inviting—choosing the route of escape, we are running away from the very place God intends to take us. It is through our struggles that God attempts to create growth in us. But He will not force it. He won't *make* us grow. And growth, frequently, is downright painful. Sometimes it downright sucks.

Take a journey with me, if you will. Back to Genesis, back to Jacob. Jacob's life begins with a struggle, even in his mother's womb. We read that he was born grasping at his twin brother's heel. His first label was 'Second Place.' Then, through the help of his mother, he slapped a new label on: 'Deceiver.' He spent much of his life deceiving, scheming, concocting his next plan to get out of whatever trouble he found himself in.

And what did Jacob do? He ran. I wonder if, during those years of running, finding himself in one mess after another, he ever stopped to daydream: "What would my life have been like if I had not deceived my father, if I had just not listened to my mother, if I had owned up to my piece of the pain in the very beginning, if I had gone to my brother to ask for forgiveness … I wonder."

How many days do we sit around and wonder, *What if…*

What if I had listened to my dad and not married her? What if I had taken that promotion? What if I had never met him?

What if I hadn't gotten in the car that night? What if I had said no instead of yes. What if … what if …

We've talked about 'owning your piece of the pain,' right? But what if there is more for you to own on this quest to discover hope and the ability to persevere?

Owning the Pain vs. Owning the Pain to Come

It's easier to accept ownership of what we have done, the problems we have caused and brought upon ourselves. I mean, it's not *easy*. But at least we have taken some steps toward identifying what pieces of our own past, of our own pain, that we can truly be held accountable for. And in doing so, we can own it.

Okay, so you've owned it—your piece of the past, the pain. "But now what?" you say. "Now you're asking me to own even more pain—pain I don't even feel yet, struggle I can't even see yet?" This is where you find yourself, much like I did and often still do, looking up and saying, "Really? Seriously?"

Think of the three children in the story The Toy Maker. Do you really think they knew what they were messing with when they fed their curiosity with every chime of the doorbell? They'd scampered down like all the other children, but they kept their distance. They just watched for a while, as if to carefully evaluate the situation before they made their move.

They were pretty happy, pretty content in their surroundings, in the orphanage. They hadn't known any differently, and well, things were okay. "If it ain't broke, don't fix it."

Oh, if they had just stayed upstairs. Up where it was safe, where it was normal, where they were comfortable. But something kept calling them downstairs. Something. Some longing for *more* that they just couldn't resist any longer. They, too, wanted to be blessed. They wanted something more. They wanted what all the other children seemingly had. So they took that fateful step forward.

They accepted the toy from the Toy Maker, who had so patiently been waiting for them to finally ask. And at last, they had their blessing, just like everyone else. Their blessing was beautiful. Their blessing brought them comfort, contentment, true happiness … beyond what they ever had before.

But sure enough, just like Jacob, just like you, just like me, what the children once saw as a blessing now seemed to shine a light on all that had been broken in them all along. Through this 'blessing,' those children began to feel emotions and encounter experiences that led them far, far outside their safe zone. Oh, if only they could close their eyes, click their red ruby heels three times, and be back in that safe corner, just watching from afar.

But that time had passed. They had grown into young adults now. They had experienced more pain in those last several years of their lives than they had ever imagined. And they now looked down at their 'blessing,' feeling shame for not recognizing it for what it was all along. And think carefully about how the Toy Maker reacted to their shame. With excitement in his voice, he just wanted to know if the children discovered the uniqueness of what he had really given them.

This casts a different light on the story. We remember the children's surprise as the Toy Maker revealed that this 'toy' they had taken for granted all these years was a *mother*. Let us for a moment imagine that the toy represented something very different from a mother. What if that 'toy' was truly a 'blessing'? We know all too well what growing pains feel like. But do you see the miracle in this blessing? Do you see the miracle in your blessing? Could this 'blessing' really be disguised as pain, as brokenness?

When I heard God tell me I would surely have cancer and I was to be happy about it, I truly thought I was going crazy. Even now, as I wait for it to come, I have hope that God will spare me from it. But what has miraculously happened is that in my waiting, I am happy. And what's more, I am not fearful.

1 Thessalonians 5:18 says, "Be thankful in all circumstances, for this is God's will for you who belong to Christ Jesus."

I am not entirely sure why my test results came back negative that day in August two years ago. But what I have come to recognize is the blessing that has been given to me as a result of my obedience to His instruction to 'be thankful in all circumstances' and to be happy. And I am more thankful for the blessing than I am even for the pain that brought it about. Let me explain. Because of my "Yes, I accept" answer, I can hear God's direction more clearly. I can see His hand in my experiences more clearly. I can feel His peace in accepting His will, even when I cannot understand it. I can have faith in His ability to 'make all things work together for my good.'

He has a lot of work left to do in me. That I am sure of. But I can be thankful, just as the Toy Maker promised, "Oh, not to worry children. I will take her back to my shop and I will fix her up, good as new. I have wonderful plans for her. Her purpose has only just begun."

The apostle Paul speaks of his weakness in II Corinthians 12. He says in verses 1-10:

1) "I must go on boasting. Although there is nothing to be gained, I will go on to visions and revelations from the Lord.
2) I know a man in Christ who fourteen years ago was caught up to the third heaven. Whether it was in the body or out of the body I do not know—God knows.

3) And I know that this man—whether in the body or apart from the body I do not know, but God knows—
4) was caught up to paradise and heard inexpressible things, things that no one is permitted to tell.
5) I will boast about a man like that, but I will not boast about myself, except about my weaknesses.
6) Even if I should choose to boast, I would not be a fool, because I would be speaking the truth. But I refrain, so no one will think more of me than is warranted by what I do or say,
7) or because of these surpassingly great revelations. Therefore, in order to keep me from becoming conceited, I was given a thorn in my flesh, a messenger of Satan, to torment me.
8) Three times I pleaded with the Lord to take it away from me.
9) But he said to me, 'My grace is sufficient for you, for my power is made perfect in weakness.' Therefore, I will boast all the more gladly about my weaknesses, so that Christ's power may rest on me.
10) That is why, for Christ's sake, I delight in weaknesses, in insults, in hardships, in persecutions, in difficulties. For when I am weak, then I am strong."

Do you think Paul had come to see this 'thorn in his side' as a blessing? He speaks of how he begged three times for God to remove this curse from him. I have to imagine that those three times didn't occur on a Monday, a Tuesday, and then again on a Wednesday. I would imagine it's more likely these three times were more like three seasons of his life.

How many seasons of brokenness are you in right now? Is this season one, season two, season 28?

My question to you is this, just like I imagine God's question to Paul may have been:

> "How many more seasons until you accept God's will for you—that He chose you to boast of nothing else but His strength, that your weakness is the catalyst to showcasing His power?"

My question to you is this, just like the Toy Maker's may have been to the three children:

> "How long will you overlook the uniqueness you've been equipped with, carefully crafted with—the uniqueness which could only have been received through this suffering?"

---

*How long will you be faithful, how long will you continue to be happy—not only **through** the pain but **for** the pain?*

My question to you is this, just as I have come to discover through the seasons of waiting for cancer to come, that God is asking of me:

> "How long will you endure, how long will you persevere, how long will you be faithful, how long will you continue to be happy—not only *through* the pain, but *for* the pain? Then, and only then, will you *see* the blessing I've already given you."

You see, I believe with all my heart that God's will is truly to bless you. And yes, in a 'good way.' In John 10:10, He tells us, "I have come so that they may have life, and that they may have it more abundantly."

During a recent conference I had attended in which I had the honor of hearing John Maxwell speak, he addressed this very verse. And for the first time in my life, I heard it much differently. Maxwell asked the audience, "What side of the comma do you want to be on—do you want life … or do you want it *more abundantly?*" What a concept, yet so easily overlooked when skimming quickly through this verse. The writer of this passage presents it in a way that it's a 'package deal.' You get life *and* you get it more abundantly.

How many of us, though, stop at 'life'? Oh, the 'more abundantly' part sounds awesome, of course. We all want that, right? Seriously, who doesn't? We want that promotion at work (more abundantly). We want that new car (more abundantly). We want to meet the 'right' man or 'right' woman and get married (more abundantly). We want to attain financial security (more abundantly). We want to see our kids get into medical school (more abundantly). We want to buy that vacation home (more abundantly).

But what if … the 'more abundantly' means something different from all those things? What if God truly wants to provide you with a blessing, but that very blessing you seek can only be found right in the midst of the storm? What if it is found right in the midst of the cancer? Found right in the midst of the divorce? Or in the midst of an abusive relationship? What if it is found right in the midst of your child's destructive choices? In the midst of your depression? Your brokenness?

My question to you in opening up this last section of this book comes with a promise. He WILL give you life more abundantly, and you WILL live on the other side of the comma, as Maxwell puts it. But first …

Will you accept this cancer?

Remember

THERE IS HOPE IN YOUR BROKENNESS

**YOU HAVE A CHOICE;
YOU ALWAYS HAVE A CHOICE**

❦

Choose to live on the **OTHER SIDE** *of the comma.
Choose to accept the* **CANCER.**

12

THE SECRET PASSAGEWAY INTO HOPE

Surrender and Forgiveness

There is a point in our lives where our feelings have the potential to begin to control us rather than us being the ones to control them. This is a dangerous and sometimes very scary place to find yourself. Maybe you know exactly what I'm talking about. It takes us to a point of depression. It takes us to a point of desperation, to a point of severe anxiety. And maybe for you, although hard to admit, it takes you to a point of searching for a way out—a way to permanently end the haunting feelings that now seem to own you.

I've been there. It was a night I will never forget.

I was lying in my bed. My three children were not with me this evening. I feared they were not safe. I feared I wasn't safe. Anxiety settled in for the night, just as I crawled under my covers. Anxiety was saying to me:

"Those kids are better off without you."

"You're nothing but a failure."

"You can't handle this."

"Just end it all, once and for all."

I had only been a few months into what would prove to be the most difficult few years of my life. My husband and I had separated, and the process of divorce had begun. My kids were a mess. I was a mess. Everyone involved was a mess. And it was sure to get messier.

I got out of my bed, grabbed my laptop, and started researching what I might have in my medicine cabinet that would bring this anxiety to an end. Something to make the voices—now relentlessly screaming at me as if they knew they had me cornered—go away. For me, it was what you might recognize as 'rock bottom.' Any inclination of hope, of success, of happiness, was crowded out by shame, by worthlessness, guilt, fear, and failure. *Just die already!* That was all I heard. Nothing but silence in my usually over-active brain. "Just die." After all, that was what I feared as the threats continued to come, promising that very thing.

That night was one of the longest nights I've ever had. I am forever grateful to my sister who talked to me on the phone for hours. She listened while I let myself really feel all I had been trying to push away, all I had been trying to ignore, to hide. It was raw. It was honest. It was exactly what I needed if I were to ever have a chance at healing, at happiness—and that night, at staying alive.

Full Surrender

After finally drifting off to sleep, I spent the next morning facedown on the floor, crying out to God. I fully surrendered. I had experienced that dangerous place where my anxiety and fear took over, and I no longer had control. I had surrendered to the names, to the labels that had been engraved in my mind, etched in my heart throughout the years, and the words and threats I had been hearing continually now for months.

But this morning was different. A new option was presented to me through my brokenness. A new kind of surrender. A surrender of my own will. I cried out that day for what seemed like hours. I don't recall eating. I don't recall ever even leaving my bedroom.

There was a new sheriff in town. And He said I was worth something. And furthermore, He said He was going to fight *for* me.

Who are you surrendering to? Who *have* you been surrendering to? How long are you going to give power to the voices of your enemy, to the people or person who has labeled you as worthless, as a failure, as an embarrassment, as a 'loser'? When is enough going to be enough?

I asked you before, "Who are you listening to?" But take it a step further, dig a little deeper. While listening to those defeating voices in your head, while you are picturing your accuser, you can clearly see the face of the one speaking those words into your heart, you can see their lips moving, you can smell their breath in your face, you experience over and over and over again the overwhelming defeat that their words bring. Have you ever stopped to consider the possibility that, in fact, you are fighting something so much bigger than you realize? And this 'one' doesn't have a recognizable face, you can't smell his breath, you can't see his lips move.

"For our struggle is not against flesh and blood, but against the rulers, against the authorities, against the powers of this dark world and against the spiritual forces in the heavenly realms."
—Ephesians 6:12, NIV

"Submit yourselves therefore to God. Resist the devil, and he will flee from you."
—James 4:7

How many times have you been in this place and you find yourself asking, "Where are you God? What have you done for me lately?"

We have this tendency to picture God as this big ferocious ruler, always looking down at us, pointing a finger, ready to inflict punishment for our sins. It's as if He's really no different from the voices of our own accusers we hear in our head. We almost begin to imagine that maybe God is the one who placed these labels on our forehead: disappointment, failure, loser.

Sticks & Stones & Once Broken Bones

I think back to a summer at the beach. It was crowded. I love the beach, but was never a fan of the beach when my kids were small. Sand stuck in diapers, seagulls swooping down at us, slapping sunscreen on every five minutes, and trying to keep a hat on a baby is just not my idea of fun, not my idea of a vacation. But this summer was a bit more relaxed. No kids in diapers. No hats needed.

While my sons paired up and ran out into the ocean with their skimboards, my daughter and I spent the afternoon digging in the sand. After a few hours of sand flying everywhere, we were both ready to plunge in the ocean. I remember neither of us being overly excited about jumping waves or going out very far. We'd just kind of get our ankles wet, maybe up to our hips if we were feeling extra adventuresome. So while she waded there looking for seashells, I headed back to my blanket. Finally, a chance to sit down and just relax, soak up some sun while I watch the kids play.

I couldn't have been sitting there for more than three minutes. I was watching the boys out there, jumping waves, having the time of their lives. My daughter, collecting shells. But wait. *Where is she?* Panic set in. I stood to my feet, now shaking. Running out to the water I frantically looked left, right, far out to the waves. Nothing. I couldn't find her pink swimming suit anywhere. The beach was crowded, very crowded. I screamed out for the boys to come in from the water. We were now all searching for her. The lifeguards were communicating with each other, looking for a little girl with light brown, shoulder-length hair, pink swimming suit.

A few onlookers were helping with the search. It felt like hours, but I am sure it was no more than a few minutes. My mind was imagining the worst. She had been taken. She had been swallowed up by the waves. Every memory I've ever shared with my little sweet girl was rushing through my mind. And suddenly, off in the distance, I saw this little pink swimming suit. She was holding the hand of the man who found her. I ran, crying tears of relief, of gratefulness I couldn't even begin to describe. Then she was in my arms. Safe.

I had told her and her brothers, "If you happen to get lost, find the closest lifeguard and just stay there. Tell them you're lost, and then just sit down and wait to be found." And that's exactly what she did. The closest lifeguard happened to be about two lifeguard towers down from where she had started picking up seashells. She had quickly drifted down the beach.

If you are a parent, I can imagine you've experienced something similar to this at least once. And if you haven't, be forewarned, you will.

What do you imagine my reaction was? Do you think I scolded her? Do you think I shamed her for straying, punished her? No, of course not. I grabbed my little girl in my arms. I held onto her so tightly. She said, "I'm sorry, Mommy. I was just getting seashells." I remember looking her in the eyes, both of us crying now, and I told her how happy I was she was okay and that I had found her. I loved her so much.

Do you really think God is any different? Do you think when we stray away from Him, His first reaction is anger when we come back? How many times have your children made mistakes? How many times, as they grew into their teenage years, have they talked back to you, disrespected you, or have thought they 'knew better' than you? Countless times. But what do you do? You continue to love them. And sure, you correct them. You guide them. But above all that, you continue to love them. Your arms are always open to them, just waiting for them to come to you.

"What does this have to do with surrender?" you wonder.

To fully surrender yourself to anything, whether it be an idea, a person, or God, you have to truly and fully trust. Trust in the validity of that idea. Trust in the character of that person. Trust in the capabilities of this God. Faith, by definition, as I shared with you earlier, is a belief that is not based on proof.

To be completely honest with you now, this may be the most difficult part of discovering hope, and of finding the strength to persevere through the storms currently brewing around you and those yet to come. How do you trust someone you can't see?

How do you fully surrender yourself and every single detail of your life—your emotions, your finances, your divorce, your loneliness, your painful past, your uncertain future? How can you possibly fully surrender when there simply is no proof? And what if you are the one sitting there, looking up to God, saying, "Where are You? What are You doing? Have You forgotten about me down here? Where exactly have You gone?"

Never Too Far

Consider the story of "The Prodigal Son." Jesus tells the story of a man who has two sons. The younger son asks his father to give him his portion of the family estate as an early inheritance. The father agrees, and the son sets off on a long journey to a distant land and begins to waste his inheritance. When the money runs out, a severe famine hits the country and the son finds himself in dire circumstances. The only job he can find is feeding pigs. Eventually, he finds himself so desperate that he is now fighting for food, alongside the pigs he is in charge of.

The son finally comes to his senses and thinks of his father. I can only imagine how foolish he feels. But with humility, he 'owns his piece of his pain' and starts the journey back to his father's house, with plans to beg for his mercy and his forgiveness, knowing all along that he is surely not worthy of it.

What do you think the father was doing? You think he had forgotten about his son this whole time? No. He had been watching and waiting, hoping for the day he'd see him walking across the field, coming back home to his open arms. And when that day finally comes, what is the father's reaction? He is overjoyed as he sees his lost son returning to him. He prepares a party! A celebration for his son, in whom he never stopped believing in, who has returned to him.

Is God any different from this father?

Does God not love you more than that father loved his own son?

And what about the Toy Maker? When those three children shamefully revealed how they had mistreated their toy all these years, what was the Toy Maker's reaction? Did he ridicule them? Did he shame them? Did he punish them for their actions? No. He listened patiently as they explained how much they loved their toy, how much comfort and love it had provided them all these years, but that they had indeed mistreated it at times, taken their anger and frustration out on it. The Toy Maker listened, allowing the children to 'own it,' but it's as if all that didn't matter. He simply wanted to know what the children had learned—if they had recognized the special feature he had designed in the toy.

And what's more, he smiled at the children. He assured them that he would fix the toy, good as new. He will repurpose the toy.

Is God any different from the Toy Maker?
Does God not love you more than even the Toy Maker loved those children?

And what of your own children?

Through the years, one of the things I repeatedly stressed to my three children was that I would always love them unconditionally. This isn't an odd thing or even a unique thing to say to your kids. I'd venture to guess that many of you have said the same thing to your own kids. But I would take it a step further and explain to them exactly what I felt that meant. It was a lot more than just something that you're *supposed* to say.

To me, it meant that I wanted them to be always honest with me. It meant that when they were angry, it was okay to tell me how they felt. It meant, if they were resentful, it was okay to tell me so. It meant, if they were confused and they didn't understand something, they should always ask me. And they believed me. They trusted me. But what this also meant was that I had willingly opened myself up to them. I had made myself vulnerable.

Remember the words of John Maxwell, "Someone doesn't care how much you know until they know how much you care."

I can remember my daughter's counselor explaining to me, "Your daughter may *seem* to hate you at times, she may lash out at you, and say hurtful things at times, sure. But it's not because she hates you. It's because she trusts you."

You see, when you truly open yourself up to loving someone unconditionally and they grow to trust that you truly do, you often become their 'safe zone.' They feel this may be the only place where they can release all their emotions, their pain … where they can feel that their feelings are valid. And so, you become that place of refuge. And often, it doesn't feel very good.

Although at times I felt very much like the toy in The Toy Maker story, never knowing if I was going to receive a great big hug or become a target for someone's bad day, I have grown to appreciate more and more the trust my children have in me. They know that I love them unconditionally.

But why do they know that? Is it because I've told them? No. Certainly not. How many times have you been told something only to find out it wasn't true? It was because I proved it to them. *Proof.*

Proof

Don't miss this. This is the big picture. My own children chose to have faith in me *before* there was proof. And as time went on, their choice to trust in me was validated because of my consistent unconditional love. They had proof long *after* they made the choice to trust me.

Remember my personal definition of 'faith'? Faith is a conscious choice we make to believe, which oftentimes develops into proof based on our own personal experience with the very thing or person we chose to have faith in.

It all begins with a choice.

Faith begins with a choice.
Surrender begins with a choice to have faith.

Faith begins with a choice. Surrender begins with a choice to have faith.

Many of us don't have that one person in our lives who we can trust to truly love us unconditionally. I am fortunate enough to have a few people in my own life like that. And although my own children are still just children, I choose to trust in them as they trust in me. But again I ask you …

Is God's love any different from the unconditional love of a mother or father?

Does God not love you more than even you love your own children?

You see, all these other discoveries we've made together through this book, while absolutely necessary, will all prove to be pointless if at this point in our journey we are unwilling to surrender.

Surrender + Humility = Forgiveness

I've shared with you this great big cloud of guilt that seems to follow me everywhere I go. It is my weakness. For me, it is that crack in the window that lets the cold air in on a winter day. It is the fracture in my bones that makes them so much more susceptible to breaking. Yes, for me, it's guilt. And yes, for me, the majority of times, it's false guilt and shame.

This is why in my own journey, this concept of surrender has been so vital. Because I desperately need freedom from this bondage of false guilt, false accusations. It doesn't matter what it is. Whether it be guilt and shame, like how it is with me. It could be anger and resentment for you. Anxiety and fear. Loneliness and worthlessness. Whatever it is—whether a combination of these things or something entirely different—it is the very thing that is causing all these tiny little fractures in our lives, that are ultimately breaking us. It might not seem like much on the surface, but underneath the skin, it doesn't look so good.

You need hope. You need strength. You need some kind of reassurance that you can make it through this storm and those yet to come. You've accepted the cancer. You've surrendered. And in doing so, you've experienced something that may very well have gone unnoticed. Humility.

No, you are not in control. No, you do not have the final say. You've given that to God. You've said, "Here you go, Lord. My life is in your hands. Now guide me. Now give me strength. Now show me the way to walk."

Maybe you've said this prayer. Maybe you've surrendered, accepted the cancer in your life and the cancer that awaits you. But God is silent. "What is He waiting for?" you wonder. "I've been faithful, I've been obedient. I've been going through this checklist of things to do in order to please You, in order to grow and learn and to change."

As we think about the Toy Maker, the father receiving into his arms his lost and wayward son, the many times you and I have welcomed back into our own open arms those we love, what is one common thing that occurs in all these stories and many more? An unspoken word, and unnoticed act? It is *forgiveness*.

They go hand in hand, surrender and humility. But what must these choices of faith ultimately result in? Yes, forgiveness.

By now, you've likely gotten a pretty clear picture in your mind of my mother. I've spent a whole chapter explaining just a few of the events of my childhood that seemed to feature my mother as the main character. You might even feel I have more than valid reasons to feel anger and resentment toward her. And you'd be right. I sure did. She failed in many ways as a mother.

It's amazing how we can find a million reasons to justify our own mistakes and failures, but we are so quick to judge others for their own. In many cases, the specifics regarding the particular mistake or failure may be exactly the same, yet we will find ourselves justifying, making excuses for why we are more deserving of forgiveness than the other person.

On January 4, 2010, I was reminded once again of how powerful the gift of forgiveness can be. I was coming home late that night, kids in tow. We had just spent the afternoon participating in an indoor soccer tournament. The kids were tired, but taking home yet another first place trophy, so they were happy. I remember pulling up to my house to see my dad's car parked there. Odd. My dad rarely came for a visit without calling first, and certainly not this late at night. I pulled into the driveway and rushed inside. He was sitting at my kitchen table all by himself, just waiting.

He didn't say a word. But his face said it all. Something was wrong. Very wrong. He immediately passed the phone to me. It was my sister, 12 hours away in her home in Tennessee. She was crying, and through her tears, I heard the words, "Amber, Mom died."

My knees buckled under me. I fell to the floor and my dad sat next to me, holding me in his arms. She was only 63 years old. How could this happen? After all she had been through this past year.

Exactly one year ago, I received a very similar phone call. "Amber, Mom's in the hospital. Doesn't look good. You better get down here." I hopped on a plane, flew down south, and spent the next few days in the hospital taking turns with other family members, going in her room to see her. I couldn't tell you exactly what her condition was. All I remember is that she wasn't communicating. No signs of her hearing or comprehending anything anyone said to her. I had spent many years resenting her, blaming her. And now she was dying.

I asked to speak to her alone. As everyone left the room, I grabbed her cold hand. She wasn't at all responsive. But I leaned in and started talking to her. "Mom," I said, "if you want to let go, you can. I'm not going to tell you to hold on like everyone else is. You can let go, it's okay." I paused for a moment, and then continued speaking to her. Still no response. "But before you let go, Mom, you have to promise me two things. You have to accept that I forgive you. I mean, I truly forgive you. I love you and I want to free you of any guilt you've been carrying all these years." As I held back tears, my tone changed. I sternly said to her, "But even more importantly, Mom, I want you to accept that God forgives you. Accept that Jesus forgave you the day He died on the cross. Accept these two things, Mom. And then you can let go if you are really ready to."

In that moment, I prayed with her. Holding her hand, I asked that God forgive her, and I asked that God forgive me for not being a better daughter to her. I asked that God spare her life if it is His will. I saw a single tear run down her cheek as I finished my prayer. I felt her squeezing my hand. She didn't say a word. Her eyes were still closed. But she heard me. And she held on.

In that last year of her life, she became a different person. She reached out to many people she had broken relationships with—her brother, her sister-in-law, her own son. And for one year of my mom's life, although she had been 12 hours away, she was the mom I had been longing for since I was a little girl, since before my parents divorced. The same mom who would sit on the couch with me and read me my favorite books over and over again. I doubt she even had to look at the words anymore, she knew them by heart. That same mom who would rock me in the big rocking chair that belonged to my grandmother. The same mom who would sit for hours and watch my painfully boring puppet shows.

I'd like to think that I had something to do with that. But in reality, I was simply the catalyst. I believe she surrendered that day in the hospital room, and I believe she accepted forgiveness, not only from me, but from God. And she found freedom from her guilt, freedom from her own painful childhood. She was free and at peace. Finally. At 62 years old.

I miss her terribly, even now as I write this. I long to pick up the phone and tell her of every milestone in my kids' lives. I long to pick up the phone and share my pain with her. Just to hear her voice. The day I offered my mom my forgiveness, I received something unexpected. In offering my forgiveness to her, I had in essence broken the chains that shackled me to the past and all those painful memories, the chains that polluted my heart with bitterness, resentment and anger. And so, I ask you ...

Did God not bleed for the faults of my mother just as he bled for mine?

Is my mother any less deserving of my forgiveness than I am of God's?

Forgive others as quickly as we expect God to forgive us

I can spend all day pointing out the wrongs of other people. And in more recent years, I can identify one person who seemed to have taken on no purpose other than to 'take me down.' The false accusations. The lies. The deceit. The manipulative schemes. The threats. At times it's been so overwhelming, as if all the other positive, reinforcing voices I hear are nothing compared to this person.

And again and again we hear God telling us to love our enemies, to forgive those who persecute us, to pray for those who seek to kill and destroy us. How? How is this even possible?

It's not easy. I won't be the one to promise you this is easy. But this is precisely why surrender and forgiveness go hand in hand. In many cases, when you are fighting against the voices of those who want nothing more than to see you suffer, it feels downright impossible to forgive them. Let's be honest, it feels near impossible to not hate them right back.

It is going to require a daily surrender to God. And by daily, I mean every single day. When you hear that alarm go off, maybe for the fifth time after hitting snooze a few too many times, before your feet even touch the ground, offer up your surrender to God. In that moment, crusty-eyed, stinky breath and all, ask Him to take control of your mind, your ears, your mouth, your eyes, your feet. In essence, allow God to take over your thoughts, to filter the voices you hear and choose to listen to, what you set your sights on, to influence the words you speak, to lead your feet down the path He has set for you that day.

If you need to stop several times during the day to humbly say this same prayer, by all means, do it. Do it every hour, every half hour if needed. Keep going. Every day. Keep going. Keep surrendering. Keep humbling yourself. And you will discover the power to forgive.

Finally—Forgiveness, Freedom.

You ask, *but what about that man or that woman or that group of people who don't deserve my forgiveness? Heck, they aren't even sorry.* And let's not forget, they continue on in their behavior and their evil schemes to destroy you. What about them? Am I supposed to forgive them too?

Forgiveness is not about approving what happened. It's not about making excuses or justifying how you've been wronged. It's simply making the choice to rise above it.

What if you took a moment to consider this person's own experiences and their own past? Consider their current pain, their current state of mind. What if instead of becoming just like them, you chose to try to understand them rather than judge them?

When another person makes you suffer, inflicts pain, imposes false accusations, and seeks to destroy you in any way they can, it is likely because deep within themselves, they are suffering too. They don't need judgement—they need help. And while you may not be the one who can provide the kind of help that person needs, perhaps what you can give them is exactly what only you can give them. *Forgiveness.* We aren't letting them off the hook for their actions; rather, we free ourselves of all the negative energy that strangles us on account of them.

Forgive ME

Sometimes the person we must forgive most is ourselves. In my own life, I find this to be true. Maybe a bit more so than the average person. But carrying false guilt and shame is no different than carrying unforgiveness in our hearts. Only the person we can't seem to forgive is ourselves.

I can assure you, people won't understand. They may even feel you're justified in the way you hold onto bitterness and resentment. But how sad to live out our lives allowing our enemies to control us like puppets. It's about time, don't you think? It's about time to release the power these voices have in your life. Let them go. Surrender. Forgive. Even if you don't feel like it, it doesn't feel sincere, just do it. Every day, do it—surrender, forgive. As the days pass by, you'll one day look back at your mindset a year ago and be amazed at what little control these voices now have. You've begun to experience the freedom that is found only in surrender and forgiveness.

Lean In

Make a list. Spell out on paper the source of those voices. Is it your ex-husband? Ex-wife? Is it your mother, your father? Is it your fourth-grade teacher? Is it your boss? Your child? Whoever it is, write their names down. Submit yourself today to forgive them. Not just once. But look at that list every day. Forgive them every day. One day, very soon, you'll find yourself able to cross people off the list.

Lean in to their pain. Lean in to their past. I chose to lean in to the pain of my mother. I chose to lean in to the pain of every person who has hurt me. And I found forgiveness, not only for their sake, but for mine as well. There are people in my life, and likely in yours as well, who you will need to lean in to their pain on a daily basis. It will take a daily surrender. You might need to bring them to God every single day. But eventually, you will find you have peace that you never had before.

If we have come to the point in our own lives that we can accept God's grace and forgiveness for us, how dare we not hold others to that same level of grace and forgiveness? How dare we judge someone else?

The voices are getting quieter now. And soon you'll hear the quiet voice of God reminding you, "There is therefore now no condemnation to those who are in Christ Jesus, who do not walk according to the flesh, but according to the Spirit."

—Romans 8:1

Remember

THERE IS HOPE IN YOUR BROKENNESS

**YOU HAVE A CHOICE;
YOU ALWAYS HAVE A CHOICE**

Choose to **SURRENDER** *and choose to* **FORGIVE** *as you have been forgiven.*

13

RACE WITH HORSES

*The Course of Persistence,
The Prize of Endurance*

There was a point in my life, I believe it was sometime after my second son was born, that I decided that *you know what, I don't want to be the 'bigger sister' anymore. I'm tired of being the chubby girl.* So I started making fitness a part of my life. I didn't really know what I was doing, but I did workout videos (yes, I said 'videos') and tried to start eating healthier. But eventually it wasn't enough. I started to discover I actually loved working out. And I was starting to feel excited about how I felt.

I enjoyed running. So naturally, I decide to enter a race. Not a 5k. Not even a 10k. Nope. I entered a duathlon. No, I hadn't gotten on a bike since I was a kid. And of course, I go all out. I get those fancy pedals with clip-in shoes. Problem is, I couldn't seem to turn my foot just right to un-clip. So over and over again, I kept falling off my bike. Just casually riding along the road, I'd come to a stop sign, and then panic. Sure enough, as if in slow motion and I couldn't stop it from happening. I'd come to a stop and my bike—and I—would fall over ever so gracefully to the right or to the left. So embarrassing. But I was just as stubborn then as I've always been. So I'd get back on, keep trying.

The running part didn't prove to be as easy or enjoyable as it used to be either. I found myself running through my neighborhood preparing for the race. I'd tell myself, just get to that next mailbox. Then, okay, just get to the stop sign. Toward the end of the few hours I spent running, I was exhausted. But I kept reminding myself that the only way to get back home to my couch and a shower was to keep going. Sure I could stop altogether and take a break on the curb, but that would make it all that much harder to get back up again. So keep running, not walking, but running. Keep going, to the next mailbox, the next stop sign, the next street. Almost there. Almost home.

When race day finally came, I was so excited. I was amazed at how many people were there for the same exact purpose as I.

Many were clearly in much better shape. There were a few that seemed lost and intimidated like I was. Then there were a few that I couldn't figure out if they were spectators or if they were really going to enter this race—by the looks of them, they surely didn't seem that they would be able to finish.

The interesting thing is, after I started the race, and had run a few miles, whenever I'd start to slow down, other runners would encourage me. They'd say, "Good job, number 927! Keep going, you've got this." Then it was time to get on my bike for the riding portion of the race. And again, "Keep it up girl, almost there! You got this, keep going." By the time I finally crossed the finish line, finishing up the running segment, I was exhausted, but I had made it. It was the most incredible feeling.

I remember that before the race started, a few fellow racers asked me how many other races or marathons I'd run. "None," I said. "This is my first race."

"What? You mean you've never even run a 5k or a 10k?"

"Nope, this is it." I've never been one to waste time on all the little steps it takes to get somewhere. If I'm in, I'm all in.

For the next few years, I ran a handful of other marathons. Each one different—either it was pouring rain, or there were hills after hills, or it was overly crowded, or the terrain was rougher than other races. But every single race brought the same indescribable rush as I approached the finish line.

You know how it is. You've counted dozens of 'just get to that mailbox, that tree, just catch up to that old lady you've been trailing behind the whole time.' Then that finish line and crowd of cheering spectators are finally in eyesight. You pick up your pace. You wipe the sweat from your face, pick up your head, push your shoulders back, and suddenly, your legs seem to find an extra surge of strength. You no longer even feel the blisters on your feet. You're almost there!

"If you have raced with men on foot and they have worn you out, how can you compete with horses?"—Jeremiah 12:5

Jeremiah 12:5 says, "If you have raced with men on foot and they have worn you out, how can you compete with horses?"

Survival of the ~~Fittest~~ PERSISTENT

Didn't I promise you that you had the power to rewrite your story? That you have the power to say this isn't how my story is going to end? I thought, like the three children, you wanted more? I thought, like Jacob, you wanted more? I thought, like me, you wanted more?

Well, do you? Do you really want more?

Isn't there a common theme you see in the story of The Toy Maker, in the many stories we read in the Bible, like Jacob, like the Prodigal Son? What about your own life? Don't you see a pattern developing? You're struggling. You see nothing but the next mailbox only half a block away. Your eyes are fixed on how tired your legs are, how dehydrated you are, how far away that couch seems. What about the 'more' you've been wanting? You don't even see it any more.

How are you going to find your 'more,' how are you going to ever run past that next mailbox if you can't keep running? It's really not that complicated. We tend to overcomplicate everything. I know I do. But in reality, it's really very simple. You want something bad enough, you will do whatever is necessary to get it. Problem is, your eyes are fixed on the next obstacle, the next roadblock, not the finish line.

Stop focusing on what you cannot do. Stop focusing on the sticks and stones. Choose to fix your focus on the finish line.

Instead of asking yourself, how much can I take? Ask yourself, how far can I go? When you started on this race, it felt a lot shorter, didn't it? When you started this race, you couldn't see the obstacles just around the corner, could you? Stop focusing on what you cannot do. Stop focusing on the sticks and stones. Choose to fix your focus on the finish line.

Anyone can give up. Giving up is the easiest thing to do. But continuing to run, pushing yourself to keep going, that is true strength—true perseverance.

I love the quote from Winston Churchill that says, "Continuous effort—not strength or intelligence—is the key to unlocking our potential."

I know what you may be thinking. "Okay, so that's a nice little story about running a marathon. But my life is a lot more difficult. You don't know the scope of my troubles. You don't see the obstacles in my path." Oh, I get it. I truly do. By no means am I trying to minimize the severity of the path you are on, let alone the difficult path that lies ahead should you decide to continue running this race.

I have to ask you, what is it that is fueling you? In other words, what is just across that finish line? *Why* are you running this race? *Who* are you running this race for? *What* is the prize you hope to receive once it's finished? These aren't questions I can answer for you. But they are certainly questions that need answering. To save your marriage? To get through the next round of chemo? To get through this semester in college? To finally get out of this town? I can't tell you what the 'it' is for you.

But I can tell you what the 'it' is for me. As for you, maybe you can relate.

It's simple. My three children. They are the *what* that's on the other side of the finish line. They are the *why* that's on the other side of the finish line. They are the *who* that's on the other side of the finish line. Since I first held my firstborn son in my arms, I knew in my heart that this was my purpose in life. To be a mother. And when I held my second son, I realized what a miracle it was to hold him. And then my daughter was born, my sweet little girl. They are my who, my what, my why.

Now comes the tough conversation. I discovered something while writing the Toy Maker story. And quite honestly, it didn't sit well with me for quite some time. It was one of the reasons I found myself in tears every single time I'd read it.

From the very beginning, that toy was created specifically for those three children. It was crafted in such a way that it would respond to those children in the exact way they needed. Obviously, this toy had a purpose. And the purpose was quite obvious. This toy was to be a mother. This toy was to be a caregiver, a nurturer, a giver, a provider.

But as the children grew into young adults, the toy seemed to no longer be of any use. The Toy Maker reassured the children that he would 'take it back to his shop, fix it up—good as new, that he had another purpose for this toy, its purpose has only just begun.' As I read this part of the story over and over again, it made me feel sad. I thought of my own children. I thought of my own place in their lives. Since I was 17 years old, I've been a mom. I've wanted nothing more than to be their mom forever. And sure, I will be. But I was starting to discover that one day, there has to be *more*.

I have kept my eyes set on them, my three children. They have been the drive that keeps me going. Each struggle they are going through becomes my 'next mailbox,' pushing me to just get to the next mailbox, to just get them through this struggle, to keep going, keep going, keep running. And every minute of the struggle, I've grown to love them more and more. I've learned to focus less and less on the tingling in my weary legs, less and less on the blisters now bleeding into my sneakers. I see the next mailbox. I see the faces of my children. I will persevere for them.

But in the last year or so, since I awoke at 3:30 a.m. to write The Toy Maker, God has opened my eyes to something greater. It's the something 'more' that I knew was out there somewhere. I just didn't know where or what it was.

What if that thing—whatever it is—on the other side of the finish line isn't at all what you thought it would be? It may be fueling you to get to that next mailbox, that next intersection, that next mile. But what if it's something more? What if on the other side of the finish line, you see, face to face, the Toy Maker? He's been patiently waiting for you to finish this race. After all, he's the one who designed the course. He's the one who knew of all the sticks and stones that would aim to obstruct the runner. He's the one who designed you with the skills to overcome the obstacles in your path. Clever and sly man, that Toy Maker.

What if He has something more for you? What if our Maker has another purpose for us?

Now, let me ask you, would you have still laced up your sneakers, would you have prepped yourself to run this race, if you had known all along that the *who*, the *what*, the *why* that you had envisioned is not at all what is on the other side of that finish line? Would you have even started the race had you known? What if you were running the race for hours, and you're almost there, would you then stop dead in your tracks and give up?

This may be unsettling for you. It was surely unsettling for me. But as I started to discover over time that my own three children, that being a mother, was not the end of my story, my only purpose in life, I began to slowly make sense of that hazy figure standing out there past the finish line. I've been running this race, it seems sometimes, like forever. Sticks and stones placed all along the path. My own damaging childhood, my failed marriage, my even more damaging divorce, let alone all that my children had suffered along the way, and as their mother, now sharing in their struggles. As soon as I figure out how to navigate the path, new sticks and stones appear out of nowhere. I thought the path had been cleared; what's the deal here?

My children will always love me. My children will always need me. But there is more. There is more for me. There is more for each of them. They have been running a race of their own. And as compared to my own youth, the course has certainly become more complex for them. The sticks are more like tree branches now. The stones are big as boulders now. And while they run their race alongside me, I will continue to encourage them, "Keep going, keep going, you can do this, you're almost there, don't give up now." And sure enough they, too, will begin to near the finish line, and they, too, will see that what lies just ahead is something more.

It may not be fame and fortune. This is no fairy tale. There is no pot of gold at the end of the rainbow. Likely, what lies just on the other side of that finish line is yet another race. But there is something very different about this next race. You see, they have run one already. And by their side, they had their toy, their mother, running alongside with them. But they have arrived. And sure enough, as they look ahead to the next race to be run, they know that this race is going to require a new perspective, a new strategy. But they have the Toy Maker now, guiding them. The Toy Maker himself through the gift of the toy over the years, throughout the course of the previous race, had strengthened these children from within.

Do you not know by now that you have a purpose? Where are you setting your sights? And when you get to that finish line, when you run through this current storm in your life, will you be willing to run another race? Will you continue to race against men, so that you will gain the endurance to race against horses? How badly do you want this? How badly do you want to rewrite your story?

Injured but Not Broken

In sharing bits of my past with you, I've given you a glimpse into my experiences. I briefly shared the physical abuse I experienced at the hand of my son's father. And again, in the previous chapter, I spoke of forgiveness. I can't conclude this chapter without again sharing a piece of this story that has inspired me.

Only a few short years after my older son was born, I received a phone call. His father had been in a car accident. He couldn't move. The voice on the other end of the line was in such distress. The doctors weren't sure if he was going to survive. A few days passed, and he became a quadriplegic. Couldn't walk, couldn't move his arms. He would be confined to a wheelchair for the rest of his life.

I can very clearly recall my own emotions at the time. I was still carrying so much anger toward him, so much bitterness and resentment. But I remember a few times visiting with him, and for brief moments, we both seemed to let our guard down. But it didn't last. He had come from his own struggles as a boy growing up. And now this? Now, the rest of his life, confined to a wheelchair? He was surely dealing with his own raging emotions of bitterness and anger.

Years passed. He was often on my mind. I had prayed for him during those years, but was it really sincere? Was I still holding onto bitterness? I certainly was. And surely, it didn't help that there were individuals, or more accurately, one individual, in my life who helped fuel that bitterness, as if my forgiving my son's father somehow posed a threat to him. It wasn't until I finally decided to begin this journey of growth and healing for myself—my own race—that I was truly able to forgive this man. I began to 'own my piece of the pain.' I began to 'lean in' to his pain. I began to see him as no different from me.

My son is a grown man now, and I have seen how his father, somehow, through the grace of God, has been able to run the race that has been placed before him. He has discovered endurance. He has embraced his suffering. I imagine, perhaps, he has seen that hazy figure out there, just beyond the finish line. And he's not sure, but he thinks it might just be the Toy Maker. And through his perseverance, he has rewritten his story.

You are going to have to make up your mind to keep running. Set your sights on the Toy Maker, just on the other side of the finish line. He has the 'more' you've been running for. Decide and choose to run the race even with the uncertainty of what exactly that 'more' is. That is faith. That is perseverance.

> "If you have raced with men on foot and they have worn you out, how can you compete with horses?"

Remember

THERE IS HOPE IN YOUR BROKENNESS

**YOU HAVE A CHOICE;
YOU ALWAYS HAVE A CHOICE**

~~~

Choose to **PERSEVERE.**
*Despite the sticks & stones in your path,
there is* **MORE.**

14

SO YOU WANNA BE A FREAK?

Persevering Through the Uncertainty

"So, you wanna be a freak?"

That was a question asked of me during a pretty heated 'discussion.' Okay, it was an argument. The last few years had brought a whirlwind of challenges. The divorce. The kids with their troubles. It had been years now, and seemingly no end in sight.

"So you wanna be a freak? Basically, you wanna eat, breathe, and sh*t God? For the rest of your life, even if you're never happy, even if you never get the things you want, the things you deserve?"

It was a question my boyfriend asked of me. Now, before I go any further, let me first explain. Not only had I been going through the most difficult season of my life thus far, but he too was experiencing it right along with me. He loved me more than I thought even possible. If you've ever loved anyone—whether a significant other or your children, you know the feeling. All you want in the world is for them to be okay, for them to be happy and to have all the things in life they deserve. You know what I'm talking about. I know what I'm talking about. It's what I feel for my own children as I watch them struggle through different seasons. Especially when I have hindsight, when I can see so clearly the path they're on and where it's leading them. But all I can do is step back and allow them to press on through it. It's the most painful, most frustrating thing in the world. You just want them to be happy.

For him, it was no different. He only wanted me to be happy. He had watched me go through this season from the beginning. We had become friends early on. And as I reflect back to those first few months, a few years ago now, I realize just how one-sided our friendship was. When I was upset, he was the one on the receiving end of my release. He was the one encouraging me, reminding me he believed in me, reminding me that God would see me through these hard times. He claims I had been an inspiration to him, even then. But surely, without his always listening ear, I don't know how I would have managed through those first several months.

When we met for coffee two summers later, it had been over a year since we had last talked. I was in a new season of my life. I was well into this race I spoke of earlier. I was growing. I was learning. Healing. And again, that summer, he found himself listening to my story of accepting the cancer I believed God would one day 'bless' me with. He struggled then to understand. It didn't make sense to him. Yet, he chose to believe in me. He chose to trust God, running alongside me through it all. We spent the next several months leaning into each other, learning of each other's stories, our dreams, our shared longing for purpose.

You see, we have always been on the opposite side of the spectrum. While I am extremely impulsive with an 'all-in' kind of mentality, he has always been very reserved. He likes to sit things out for a bit, really think things through, maybe sometimes to a fault. But this time, as he observed all he was getting himself into, thinking this might be a good time to run the other direction, he felt God speaking to him. He heard Him reassure him, "I have this woman for you, Brian. She's not what you were looking for. She's not simple. Her life is very complicated. But she is going to be good for you. Trust Me." And so he did. We sat on a park bench that day when he told me he wanted to open his heart up to me. That he had no idea how to handle all the complications I came with, but that he was willing to try, that he believed there was something about me that was just right.

Sounds like a sweet guy, right? So why such a harsh question, why such a harsh accusation? It was tough to swallow for sure. I remember hearing those words; they cut deep. And I thought, "Well, yeah, I do wanna be a freak, I guess." For over a year now, he had been by my side. Through each and every pot-hole in the road, he had been running this race alongside me. For him, it was the first race of this magnitude. For me, I had been running these marathons for a very long time. I knew the turns; I knew the terrain. But this was all new for him. And all he wanted was to get to the end of the race. He was tired. He was dehydrated. And dammit, he just wanted to grab my hand and cross that finish line together.

There are moments in this race that you will start to question why you are running so hard in the first place. Why run at all? Look at the spectators. Why not be one of them? Or look at the guys pouring cups of water for the runners as they pass by. Why not be one of them? Why in the world run this race if, at any time, you have the option to hop off the course and just do something else? The spectators play a very helpful role: they cheer the runners on. The volunteers have a purpose: to offer rehydration to the runners. These are all very important, very necessary parts to any race. Why not jump off and choose a simpler role? Why in the world do you *choose* to run this race? It is hard. It is oftentimes painful, leaving blisters, sore muscles, and sometimes along the way, you encounter injury that sets you back. And yet, you get back on the course. Why?

I believe this is really what burned in his mind that day. Why was I choosing to run this race? I've been running a long time. I deserved a break. I deserved to just volunteer in some way on the sidelines, help someone else along. But why me, why was I still on this road?

But during this race, I had heard of this Toy Maker standing on the other side of the finish line. I knew he was there, waiting for me. I knew he had a greater purpose for me. He told me so that day I sat at the Global Leadership Summit. There *was* more. And I was determined to keep on running. To some, that makes me a bit freakish, I'd imagine.

I think of the man I mentioned earlier, whom I had met with. I think of him referring to me as the 'white-picket-fence' girl. I think of the women I've been able to reach through my personal training business, all the while hearing ridicule because I 'couldn't even make $10,000 that year.' I think of my son in college, as he shares with me how he's been helping a friend through a disease she's been fighting and how he's shared with her some of my story and the things he says to encourage her. I think of my other son, who texts me just to tell me he's proud of me and he believes I'm going to do great things. I think of my daughter, who I hear brags about her mom to other people.

Then I think way back to the stories we've all heard in the Bible. The Old Testament stories of perseverance: Noah spending 120 years building an ark for rain that he had no proof would come—FREAK. Abraham was 100 years old when his promised son was born, only to hear God instruct him to sacrifice him—FREAK. Moses dedicated most of his life to rescuing God's chosen people, only to never see the promised land himself—FREAK. Jacob worked 12 years to marry the woman of his dreams, only to be deceived into marrying her ugly sister, then work another 12 years for the woman he had wanted—FREAK.

And what about the New Testament? You think the followers of Jesus weren't called 'freaks'? If you think you are alone running this race, if you think you alone are being ridiculed, being called crazy or a freak, think again.

God does not call us to be perfect.
He calls us to be dependent.

But what do all of these characters of old have in common? Faith. Hope. Perseverance. But they all had a choice. They all chose to run the race set before them. There were detours at every single turn. And sometimes they took them. Sometimes we take them. But we always have the choice to get back on the road and run. We will make mistakes. We will get off course. There isn't a character in the Bible, other than Jesus Himself, that didn't jump ship from time to time. God does not call us to be perfect. He calls us to be dependent. How? By keeping our eyes set on the finish line, that hazy figure we'll see waiting for us.

Something has changed in the current year of my life. I am no longer running this race to reach the prize at the end of the finish line. I'm running this race because of the pretty, popular girl in my study hall. Remember her? I mentioned her early on in this book. I asked you to tuck her away in the back of your mind, that I'd get back to her. She did something so small, seemingly so insignificant. And while it has been many years since I sat at a desk in high school, this girl is on my mind. I wonder how many times before I came to surrender my life to God, she had been tucked away in the back of my mind, reminding me I'm worth something? I'm worth her time, I'm worth the teasing she would receive for sitting with me. I'm worth 45 minutes of her day.

This is why I run. This is why I choose to be a freak.

I've been called a hypocrite. You will too. Why? Because you will make mistakes. You will fall short of your own standards. You will fail. But do you know how many people in my life seem to remind me of this? One. Do you know how many people I've heard thank me for encouraging them? Many. I'm not saying any of this to draw attention to myself, to puff my chest up and show off how great I am. No. Quite the opposite. I am telling you that I am weak. I still hear those condescending, ridiculing, mocking voices in my head. It's a daily battle to decide which voice I'm going to listen to. But just like I needed that pretty and popular girl to fill me with hope, I wish to fill even one other person with hope.

This is why I run. This is why I choose to be a freak.

This course is not going to be an easy one. It is full of potholes. It will oftentimes storm—rain, hail, snow, you name it. It will frequently present itself with hurdles, obstacles to overcome. But with each passing storm, with each passing obstruction, you will discover something amazing, something powerful. You *do* have the power to become the author of your own story. And along the way, you *will* find hope. But you must keep running. You must persevere. Why? Because there is *more*.

My boyfriend wanted nothing more than for me to be happy, for us to be happy, to have all we 'deserve' in this life. And in the course of this race he's been running alongside me, he too has begun to discover that there truly is more. More than what he thought, more than what he had hoped for. And so yes, I stand and say, I am a freak. I am proud to be a freak.

I invite you, my friend, to run alongside me. You will have spectators watching you, no doubt. Some of them may cheer you on. But rest assured, there will be ones along the way that you'll see out of the corner of your eye—sticks in hand, stones in hand, throwing them up ahead, right in your path. Never mind them. At times they may be the only ones you see, the only voices you hear. But remember who you are. Remember that the Toy Maker designed you with very special features—features you may not discover until you need them the most, until the terrain gets really rough. Remember that pretty girl in high school—we all have one of those. Use her to remember who you are—that you are worth it.

And above all, remember that there is *more* just across that finish line.

Choose to be a FREAK.

Respond with Yes when you'd rather say No.
Persevere against all odds.
Give when it's easier to take.
Sacrifice with no guarantee of gain.
Believe you can when they say you can't.
Relinquish control in times of uncertainty.

This will make you a freak. This will paint a picture of 'crazy.' But hold your head high.

You are almost to the finish line. Keep running, you freak! I'm right there with you!

Remember

THERE IS HOPE IN YOUR BROKENNESS

YOU HAVE A **CHOICE**;
YOU **ALWAYS** HAVE A CHOICE

⤞⤝

Choose to be proud to be a **FREAK** *in this world.*

Part V

THE THREE CHILDREN

My Three Children

I began this book asking you, "What breaks your heart?" I cannot hold up my end of the bargain and conclude this book without answering my own question to you.

What breaks my heart?

Remember when I asked you this question, it was not to discover what makes you sad. It was to discover what your purpose is. What matters to you. Where your heart resides.

To my three children, Justin, John, and Julia:

I love you. YOU are where my heart resides. Each of you holds a special, irreplaceable place in my heart that is unique—apart from one another. I've told you over and over again that my love for you is unconditional. It will be consistent, no matter the circumstances, no matter the season you find yourselves in. I could write another three books just explaining all the ways I love each of you. But you all already know that. What is most important to me and what I hope for you, is that you will one day open your hearts to God. To come to know Jesus in the way that I have. I will always love you, yes. But one day, just like the three children in the Toy Maker story, you will venture out into the world, all grown up. I want you to carry in your hearts the love I have for you, but even more than that, the love of the Toy Maker—our God. I want you to run the race set before you with perseverance. But I want you to run knowing you are never running alone. The road may be hard sometimes; the terrain may be rough. But my wish for you is that you will find what breaks your own heart. I want you to live your life with purpose. I want you to live every day with intention. I want you to love, as God loves you. I want you to forgive, as God forgives you. I want you to persevere, as God will enable you to. I want you to know that I believe in you. That I am proud of you. That when no one else in the world seems to believe in you, I do. You three children have been my inspiration. Your big hearts are like none other. I am so thankful for every single moment I've been blessed to be your mother. I love you, Justin. I love you, John. I love you, Julia.

Love, Your Mom

ACKNOWLEDGMENTS

TO MY FAMILY
Justin, John and Julia—my children
John Groover—my dad
Nick and Heather Joy—my sister and her husband
Mark Meyers—my brother
And my mom—Priscilla Smith

TO MY DAD, JOHN H. GROOVER JR:
Thank you, Dad, for showing me what it means to love as Christ, loves. You've consistently shown me unconditional love and support. I could not have asked for a better earthly father. I love you.

TO BRIAN MICHAEL SAVARY:
Thank you for always believing in me. You will forever be in my heart.

THE FREELANCERS
William K. Weber—Copy Editor/Proofreader and friend
Danielle Reardon—Photographer and friend

THE SUPPORTERS, FRIENDS, AND ENCOURAGERS
Kary Oberbrunner, Brian Savary, Mike & Nancy Savary, Travis 'the Featherhawk' Snyder, Larry Bonino, Bill White, Kelly Essig, Jean Natale, Julie Burkey, Michael Barrovecchio, Dena Bowling, Benjamin Hampton, Jenifer Lee, Tim & Diana Calhoun, Jeff &

Amber Noelle

Danielle Zenz, Gary Seibert, Jeremy Torres, Dawn Savary, Casey Redner, Dean Rogers, Sonia Marchio, Sam Albert

THE CHALLENGERS
John C. Maxwell, Andy Stanley, Charles Stanley, Max Lucado, Nick Vujicic, Paul Martinelli, Kary Oberbrunner
The Author Academy Elite Tribe *and The* John Maxwell Team

NOTES

WARNING: This is Going to Hurt
1. dictionary.com, Perception— noun: the act or faculty of perceiving, or apprehending by means of the senses or of the mind; cognition; understanding.

A Trip Down Memory Lane
1. John C. Maxwell bio and quote: "People don't care how much you know until they know how much you care." johnmaxwell.com

One Common Denominator
1. Northpoint Community Church series "Starting Over" by Pastor Andy Stanley. northpoint.org/messages/starting-over/ "Your best bet at a successful future is owning your piece of the past."
2. Brene Brown quote: "Owning our story and loving ourselves through the process is the bravest thing that we will ever do." http://www.goodreads.com/quotes/330217-i-now-see-how-owning-our-story-and-loving-ourselves

False 'Facts'
1. John Moore quote: "Your opinion is your opinion. Your perception is your perception. Do not confuse them with facts or truth." http://www.notable-quotes.com/p/perception_quotes.html

2. Mark Twain quote: "Education consists mainly of what we have unlearned." http://www.twainquotes.com/Education.html

Race with Horses

1. Winston Churchill quote: "Continuous effort—not strength or intelligence—is the key to unlocking our potential." http://www.brainyquote.com/quotes/quotes/w/winstonchu385862.html

BRING AMBER INTO
YOUR ORGANIZATION, BUSINESS OR EVENT

AUTHOR
SPEAKER
TRAINER
LIFE COACH

Amber Noelle is an author, speaker, trainer and life coach.

She is a certified member of the John Maxwell Team, lead by John C. Maxwell—the #1 leader in business by the AMA and the world's most influential leadership expert by Inc.

Amber dedicates her life to pursuing her passion—to inspire broken, hurting people to find hope in their brokenness and to tap into the power to persevere against all odds. She believes in living an intentional life, a life with purpose—on purpose.

Amber is a mom to three amazing children. She believes she has been blessed with her struggles for one single purpose—to ignite the power of perseverance. Amber is also a Creative Marketing Professional and a Certified Personal Trainer.

CONTACT AMBER TODAY TO START THE CONVERSATION
AMBER-NOELLE.COM

If this book has had a positive impact on you, please share your story with Amber. She would love to hear from you. Email her directly at an@amber-noelle.com.

Made in the USA
Charleston, SC
13 February 2017